EXPLORING DEBATE 1

Jack Clancy **Sean Bienert**

contents

Book 1

How would my life be different without television?

Is dieting necessary?

UNIT 01 Fast Food ... 5

UNIT 02 Dieting ... 11

UNIT 03 Watching TV ... 17

UNIT 04 School Life ... 23

UNIT 05 Cosmetic Surgery ... 29

UNIT 06 Family ... 35

UNIT 07 Pets ... 41

UNIT 08 Valentine's Day ... 47

Which is more important; how a person looks or how a person acts?

UNIT 09	Internet Anonymity ... 53
UNIT 10	Success and Happiness ... 59
UNIT 11	Pollution ... 65
UNIT 12	Peer Pressure ... 71

Is anonymity good or bad for the internet?

UNIT 13	Children Studying Abroad ... 77
UNIT 14	Corporal Punishment ... 83
UNIT 15	The Lottery ... 89
UNIT 16	Gap between Rich and Poor ... 95

Is corporal punishment effective?

UNIT 17	Modern Life ... 101
UNIT 18	Animal Testing ... 107
UNIT 19	Online Gaming ... 113
UNIT 20	Role Models ... 119

Online gaming; beneficial or harmful?

UNIT 1 Fast Food

ED1-01
MP3

Warm-up

🟠 Fill in the circles with foods that you can order in a fast food restaurant.

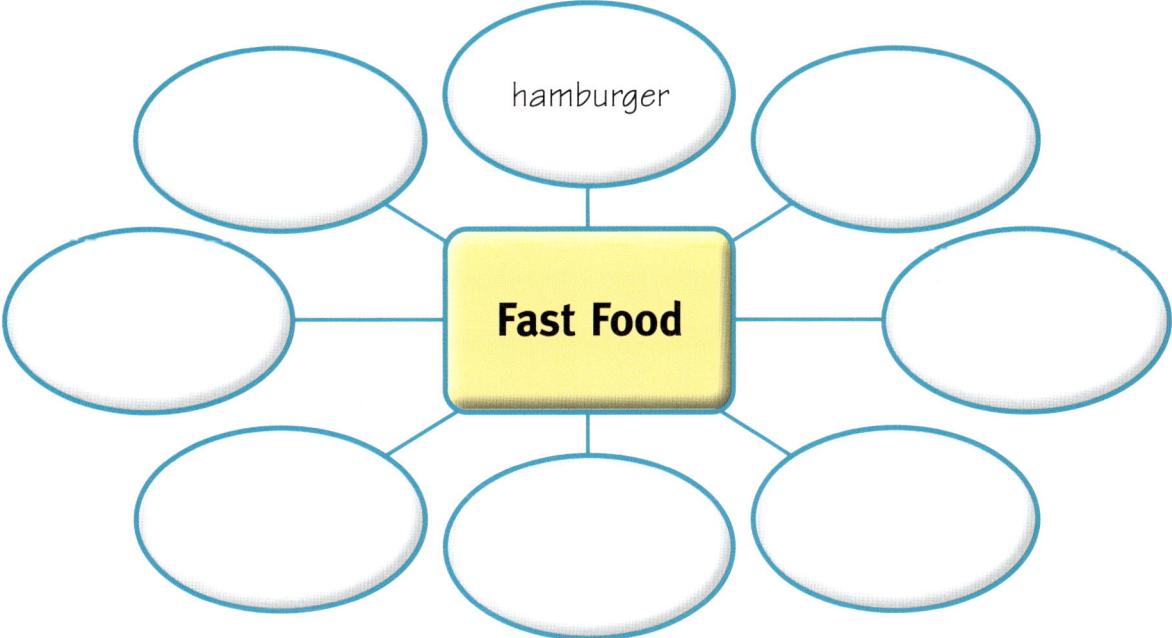

🟠 Interview a classmate using the questions below.

1. What's your favorite fast food restaurant?
2. How often do you eat fast food?

Fast Food

🔴 **Read the passage.**

Track 1

Fast food is not a new idea. It began when people started to live in cities, like ancient Rome. Many people could not afford a place to live that had a kitchen. Instead, they went to small, cheap and fast restaurants on the street for a simple meal. Bread, wine and noodles were popular and simple dishes.

Now, fast food is different. Almost all of us have a kitchen where we can prepare our own food. However, fast food restaurants are more popular than ever! We can see them all over our cities. Today, fast food is processed in a factory and brought to restaurants in trucks. Then, it is assembled and reheated when you order. Many people believe that fast food is not healthy food. Fast food is high in fat but low in fiber. It has too many calories and is served in very large portions. For these reasons, fast food is a major cause of obesity. Obesity causes diabetes and heart disease. This is a serious problem in the United States where 20% of the population is obese.

Despite the problems of fast food, the industry continues to grow. In countries like India, the fast food industry grows 40% every year. Even though we know it's not very good for us, we all crave fast food sometimes. It's important to think about what we eat if we want to be healthy. For these reasons, we should carefully examine our fast food culture.

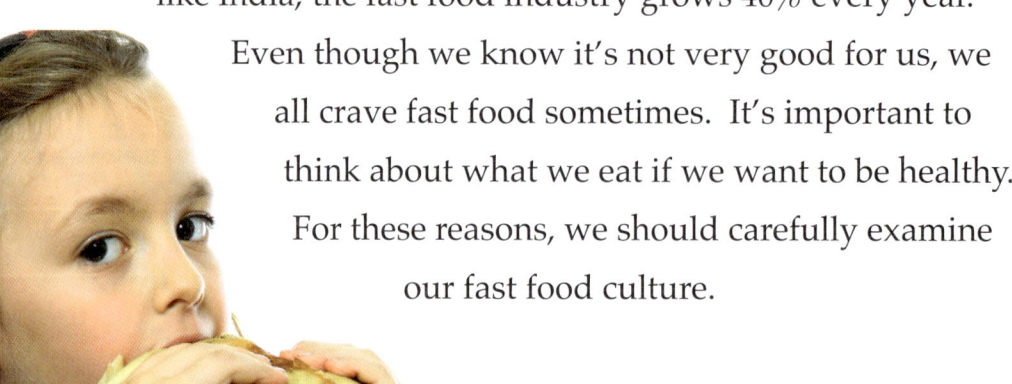

Comprehension Check — Answer the questions.

1. When did fast food begin?
2. Where is fast food made?
3. What does fast food not have enough of?
4. How fast is the fast food industry growing in India?
5. What health problems are caused by eating fast food?

Vocabulary Check — Complete each sentence with a word from the box.

| despite | industry | obesity | examine | crave |

1. "I like to eat fast food, _____ the fact that it's unhealthy."
2. The oil _____ makes a lot of money every year.
3. Doctors often _____ their patients.
4. _____ is the condition of being extremely overweight.
5. Sometimes we don't understand why we want something, we just _____ it.

Think About It

Think about the advantages and disadvantages of fast food.

Advantages
- Quick service
-
-

Disadvantages
- Not enough fiber
-
-

7

Opinion Practice

● **Practice supporting/refuting the opinions.**

Supporting Opinions

1. Fast food is not healthy... _____
2. People are becoming more obese today... _____
3. It is easier for busy families to eat fast food... _____
4. Fast food is more fun than cooking... _____

> a. because you can get toys and eat with your friends.
>
> b. because it is cheap and very fast to make.
>
> c. because they eat food in very large portions which is also high in calories.
>
> d. because it is high in fat and low in fiber.

Refuting Opinions

1. It takes too long to cook at home. _____
2. Eating fast food will make you obese. _____
3. It is too expensive to make dinner. Fast food is cheaper. _____
4. Fast food tastes better than the food I eat at home. _____

> a. That's not necessarily true! Many meals can be made quickly and are very easy to prepare.
>
> b. That's easy to solve! Buy a cookbook and teach yourself to cook. There are many delicious recipes and many different types of food to try.
>
> c. That's not always true. Many meals can be made very cheaply. Often it can be cheaper to cook at home.
>
> d. Only if you eat too much and do not exercise. If you live a healthy lifestyle and eat only a little fast food you will not necessarily become obese.

Opinion Examples

- Read the opinions and answer the questions.

Opinion A

Track 2

❝ I like fast food restaurants because they're fun. Hamburgers and french fries are more fun to eat, because you eat them with your hands. People are friendly and the colors are bright. My mom and dad take me to a fast food restaurant to cheer me up when I'm in a bad mood. They know I enjoy the cheerful atmosphere. If they took me to a quiet, boring, slow restaurant it would only make me feel worse. ❞

Opinion B

Track 3

❝ I don't think fast food is real food. It looks, smells and tastes very different from the food my mother makes. Also, after I eat fast food, I don't feel well. It makes me slow and heavy. I read that fast food has a lot of fat but no fiber. I think fresh food is important. So when I'm busy and don't have time to prepare my own meals, I bring some simple food with me. Apples and nuts, or a banana and some raisins are portable and healthy to eat. ❞

1. Please circle the main idea in each opinion.

2. Please underline the supporting ideas in each opinion.

3. What would you say to further support the opinion with which you agree?

Discussion Questions

● **Discuss the questions in groups.**

1. Should fast food chains be allowed to advertise to children? Why or why not?

2. What do you think about all the trash that fast food restaurants create?

3. What are the advantages of fast food restaurants?

4. Why do you think fast food restaurants are so popular?

5. What is an example of healthy food? Name the food and explain why it is healthy.

Expression Tips

Beginning of Discussion/Debate
All right. Shall we start?
First of all, let's discuss ~
Let's talk about ~

Choose one statement. Debate the statement in groups.
(One group agrees with the statement, the other group disagree with the statement.)

1. Fast food chains should be prohibited from serving unhealthy food.

2. Fast food is a necessary evil.

3. We should ban fast food advertising to children.

UNIT 2 Dieting

MP3

Warm-up

- Put numbers in the blanks that show their order of importance to a person's health. "1" is the most important, "10" is the least important.

  _____ eating fruits and vegetables

  _____ chewing your food

  _____ exercising regularly

  _____ not having too much stress

  _____ getting enough sleep

  _____ chewing gum

  _____ being the best computer game player

  _____ being stronger than your friends

  _____ being on time to appointments

  _____ getting along with your friends

- Interview a classmate using the questions below.

  1. Have you ever been on a diet?
  2. Can you list some foods you think are healthy?

Dieting

● **Read the passage.**

Track 4

Most doctors and health professionals say that the two most important factors in our health are diet and exercise. This does not mean to begin dieting. "Diet" and "dieting" are two different terms. Dieting is when people change their diet only for a short time. Usually, this is to lose weight. A person's diet is what they eat in their day to day life. So, what doctors mean is for people to "eat healthy and exercise."

When someone starts dieting, they often reduce the amount of food they eat in order to lose weight for a certain amount of time. There are a lot of problems with this. Often, when a person goes on a temporary diet, as soon as they stop, they often gain the weight back. Some people have unrealistic body images - mostly created by what they see in the media. This can cause the illnesses, bulimia and anorexia. Bulimia is when a person vomits after eating to prevent the calories from causing them to put on weight. Anorexia is when a person stops eating altogether. Both of these are very serious problems and can even kill a person if they do not get help.

Eating disorders are unhealthy, and dieting often leads to disappointment because it doesn't work. There isn't even anything wrong with eating junk food every now and then. The important thing is to remember moderation. The best way to stay in shape is eating a balanced diet and exercising regularly.

Comprehension Check Answer the questions.

1. What are some illnesses caused by dieting?
2. What happens if we go on temporary diets?
3. What happens to a person suffering bulimia?
4. According to the passage, what can we do to have a healthy body?
5. What does dieting often cause and why?

Vocabulary Check Complete each sentence with a word from the box.

| stay in shape | vomiting | unrealistic | reduce | moderation |

1. I have the flu, so I was up _____ all night.
2. It is _____ to expect children to sit quietly that long.
3. You're driving too fast! Please _____ your speed.
4. I bought an exercise bike to _____.
5. Drinking is not harmful if you do it in _____.

Think About It

Think about the advantages and disadvantages of dieting.

Advantages
- Dieting can improve your confidence.
-
-

Disadvantages
- Dieting doesn't give your body enough nutrients in some situations.
-
-

Opinion Practice

- **Practice supporting/refuting the opinions.**

Supporting Opinions

1. People should change their diets if they are overweight... _____
2. Dieting is bad... _____
3. For most people, it is important to exercise... _____
4. People diet for the wrong reasons... _____

> a. because if you don't, you can put on fat.
>
> b. because being overweight is bad for your health.
>
> c. because people usually gain weight right back after they finish the diet.
>
> d. because they want to look like the people they see on TV.

Refuting Opinions

1. Not eating is a fast way to lose weight. _____
2. You should change your diet to look like your favorite celebrity. _____
3. It is not necessary to exercise to lose weight. _____
4. I am thin so I can eat anything I want! _____

> a. That may be true, but it is also unhealthy and very dangerous!
>
> b. I disagree. The best way to lose weight is to eat healthy food and exercise regularly.
>
> c. That's a bad idea. You should diet to be healthy, not to look like other people.
>
> d. That's not true. If you eat too much unhealthy food, you can still have health problems.

Opinion Examples

Read the opinions and answer the questions.

Opinion A

Track 5

❝ Dieting has helped me to gain self-confidence. When I was overweight, my clothes did not fit and I was often out of breath if I had to run or climb stairs. I was embarrassed to go to the beach or play sports. Since I've begun dieting and exercising, I am much happier with my body. I feel good about myself and I am a healthier person. Now that I've lost weight I have confidence that I can do anything. ❞

Opinion B

Track 6

❝ Dieting is useless. Most people who go on diets to lose weight only succeed for a short time. They change their eating habits for a short period of time and then go back to eating the way they always did. There is no easy answer to being thin and healthy. Diets make us believe that if we follow some special rules for a few weeks, we can be fit and happy. That's not the way our bodies work. We need to avoid junk food all the time and concentrate on eating fresh fruits and vegetables if we want to be healthy. ❞

1. Please circle the main idea in each opinion.
2. Please underline the supporting ideas in each opinion.
3. What would you say to further support the opinion with which you agree?

Discussion Questions

● **Discuss the questions in groups.**

1. Have you ever been on a diet? Please tell your group about your experience.

2. Why do you think dieting is so popular?

3. Why do you think diet books and programs are such a big business?

4. Do you think all diets work? Why or why not?

5. Would you ever advise a friend to go on a diet? Why or why not?

Expression Tips

Beginning of Discussion/Debate

Okay, let's begin our discussion on ~

Today, we're going to talk about ~

Today's discussion will be on ~

Choose one statement. Debate the statement in groups.
(One group agrees with the statement, the other group disagree with the statement.)

1. People diet because they want to look like the people on the TV.

2. Most diets don't work.

3. Dieting is necessary for many people.

UNIT 3 Watching TV

Warm-up

- **Fill in the chart with TV programs you like or not.**

I like to watch	Because
Evening news	I can see what's happening right now.

I don't like to watch	Because
Professional wrestling show	They're too violent.

- **Interview a classmate using the questions below.**

  1. How much time do you usually spend watching TV each day?
  2. How many televisions do you have in your house?

Watching TV

🔸 **Read the passage.**

Watching TV is something that nearly all of us do, but it wasn't always that way. The television has only been around for less than one hundred years and only widespread in any country for about sixty years. We do not often examine the effects television has had on our cultures and lifestyles. However, everyone can agree that television has had an enormous effect. TV influences the way we dress and the songs we listen to. It shapes our ideas and opinions about the world we live in.

Television allows us to have greater access to the larger world. We can learn about places, people and things that we would normally not be able to learn about. TV has become our window on the world.

However, there are some negative effects of television. First, there is a connection between obesity and TV viewing. The more we watch TV instead of being active, the fatter we get. Also, TV exposes us to a lot of images of violence. Some studies show that children who watch violent television shows become more violent people. Also, television has a lot of commercials. These encourage us to buy more and more things. Some people find these commercials annoying.

Lastly, TV is a powerful tool for spreading messages and stories. When we watch TV, we begin to accept those messages even if we don't realize it. Should we really let someone else control our thoughts?

Comprehension Check Answer the questions.

1. For how long has the television been popular?
2. What are some ways television influences us?
3. Why is violence on TV a bad thing?
4. What is another negative effect of television?
5. According to the passage, what is TV used for?

Vocabulary Check Complete the sentence with a word from the box.

| examine | effect | influence | annoying | expose |

1. You should _____ the facts very carefully.
2. Extra studying has had a big _____ on your grades.
3. In life, some things can be frustrating and _____.
4. Don't _____ yourself to the sun, or you'll get burned.
5. Your parents, school and friends all _____ the way you think.

Think About It

Think about the advantages and disadvantages of TV watching.

Advantages
- Gives us information about the world
-
-

Disadvantages
- Can lead to obesity
-
-

19

Opinion Practice

- **Practice supporting/refuting the opinions.**

   Supporting Opinions

   1. Watching TV can be a great way to learn... _____
   2. TV has had a big influence on society... _____
   3. Watching too much TV is bad... _____
   4. TV encourages us to buy more... _____

   > a. because we see many advertisements in commercials.
   >
   > b. because it has changed the way we communicate and it lets us see other parts of the world from our home.
   >
   > c. because we can get a variety of information much faster than reading a book.
   >
   > d. because it makes us inactive and can lead to obesity.

   Refuting Opinions

   1. People who watch TV will be obese. _____
   2. TV is bad because all of the programs are too violent. _____
   3. I must have a television to hear the news. _____
   4. People were always bored before the television was invented. _____

   > a. On the contrary. Before TV, people entertained themselves by reading, playing sports and using their imagination.
   >
   > b. Some are violent, but not all. Many shows are fun and educational.
   >
   > c. That's not necessarily true. If you exercise, eat good food and only watch a little TV you will not become obese.
   >
   > d. You can find the news many ways. You can read a newspaper or go on the internet.

Opinion Examples

● Read the opinions and answer the questions.

Opinion A

Track 8

❝ I think that television makes people dull. Television affects us when we watch it. It doesn't matter what we watch, the effect is the same. We stop thinking, and just take in what we're told. We don't have to make decisions or express thoughts. We just listen. Over time we could forget how to speak well, and our minds could become lazy. When we interact with other people, our eyes are bright, we move and look alive. I think that if you watch too much TV, you'll become stupid and unable to interact with others. ❞

Opinion B

Track 9

❝ Watching television is very educational. When we go through the channels we can see many events and cultures from around the world. If it wasn't for the television, I couldn't watch sports from far away or keep up on current events on other continents. I can also watch shows where I learn about nature. Television shows are also very short, so I can learn only the important things in a short period of time. I learn many things on television in just half an hour. It would be very difficult for me to learn all those things at the library. ❞

1. Please circle the main idea in each opinion.

2. Please underline the supporting ideas in each opinion.

3. What would you say to further support the opinion with which you agree?

Discussion Questions

● **Discuss the questions in groups.**

1. How do you think people spent their time before television?

2. Could you go for a week without watching television? Why or why not?

3. How would your life be different without television?

4. Would life without television be a positive or negative thing? Please explain your answer.

5. How do you feel about commercials on TV? Give an example.

Expression Tips

Beginning of Discussion/Debate

We're here today to talk about ~

What we want to do today is to discuss ~

Today's topic of discussion is ~

Choose one statement. Debate the statement in groups.
(One group agrees with the statement, the other group disagree with the statement.)

1. Television is an important educational tool.

2. Television is an advertising tool.

3. Television is only a source of entertainment.

UNIT 4 School Life

Warm-up

- Fill in the chart with people, subjects, and facilities you can see in a school.

School		
People	**Subjects**	**Facilities**
teachers	math	hallway

- Interview a classmate using the questions below.

  1. Describe something positive that happened in school this week.
  2. Describe something negative that happened in school this week.

School Life

● **Read the passage.**

Track 10

School is an important part of our lives. Most of us begin when we are little children and go until we are at least eighteen. Our education plays a big part in what we will do and who we will become as adults. When we are young, we go to school to learn basic skills. We learn to get along in a group and make friends.

Competition is a big part of school. We try to get the best marks so that we can be at the top of our class. Is competition a good thing to learn? Some people believe it's better to learn how to cooperate. That way, we learn to solve the world's problems together. Cooperation may be one of the most important skills we can learn.

Some children stay at home instead of going to school. Their parents help them learn without a classroom. Other experts may teach them as well. This is called home-schooling. They don't have to compete with anyone. They have education with no buzzers and no competition. They learn to ask questions and teach themselves. For them, the whole world is a classroom.

Education can happen in many different ways. In Finland, young school children may not get official grades. In Canada, high school students can study outside for several months and learn about nature.

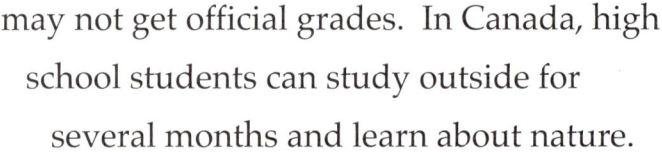

You will never stop learning. School is just the beginning of a lifetime education. There is so much to discover in the world. Your school can give you the tools to go out and discover it.

Comprehension Check — Answer the questions.

1. What's one of the main purposes of going to school when we are young?
2. What can we learn instead of competition?
3. How is home-schooling different?
4. Why do some people believe that cooperation is better?
5. Why is school an important part of our lives?

Vocabulary Check — Complete the sentence with a word from the box.

get along	mark	compete	official	buzzer

1. I'm very friendly and I _____ with everybody at school.
2. I just heard the _____ ring, so it's time to go for lunch.
3. Your grades are written on your _____ report card.
4. I got a low _____ on my history exam.
5. We will _____ against the other team in soccer.

Think About It

Answer the questions.

1. If you could study anything you want, what would you choose to learn about?

2. According to the passage, "you will never stop learning." Do you agree or disagree? Why or why not?

3. Are you a good student? At what subject are you successful? What subject is difficult for you?

Opinion Practice

● **Practice supporting/refuting the opinions.**

Supporting Opinions

1. Studying at home is better than being in a classroom... _____
2. It is better to be in a classroom than studying at home... _____
3. It is important to learn basic skills when you are young... _____
4. It is important to cooperate... _____

> a. because you can learn with your friends.
>
> b. as we need to be prepared for life as adults.
>
> c. so that we can work together to solve problems.
>
> d. because there is no competition or pressure from other students.

Refuting Opinions

1. You do not need to go to school. The information is useless anyway. _____
2. School is boring. It is much more fun to play. _____
3. Cooperation is more important than competition. _____
4. You must study the same way as your friends. _____

> a. School can be very fun and exciting. For example, you can go to school to learn how to fly a plane!
>
> b. There are many different ways to study, and it is important to find the best way for you.
>
> c. That's not true. You need to learn basic skills to prepare for life as an adult.
>
> d. Both are important. Competition can help us to work harder and be our best.

Opinion Examples

- Read the opinions and answer the questions.

Opinion A

Track 11

❝ School is no fun. We are forced to go there nearly every day for many years. When we could be outside playing or still in bed, we sit in a classroom and learn boring stuff. I know that it's important to learn how to read and write, but does it really take so long? I also think we learn lots of useless things that aren't practical in our daily lives. Why should I learn about math or history when I will never need to know them? I can hardly wait until high school is over and I can spend my time the way I want. ❞

Opinion B

Track 12

❝ Every morning I wake up and I am excited about going to school. I can't wait to get there and meet my friends, open my locker and get my books. Without school I wouldn't be able to learn so many wonderful things and do so many interesting activities. In my school, I'm involved in the chess club, the swim team and student government. If there were more hours in a day I would join more clubs and teams. I like school so much that I want to be a teacher when I grow up. ❞

1. Please circle the main idea in each opinion.

2. Please underline the supporting ideas in each opinion.

3. What would you say to further support the opinion with which you agree?

Discussion Questions

● **Discuss the questions in groups.**

1. How would you spend your time if you did not go to school?
2. How would your life be different if you could not read or write?
3. What are some valuable things that you learn in school?
4. What would you like to learn about that is different from school subjects?
5. Why is it important to get an education?

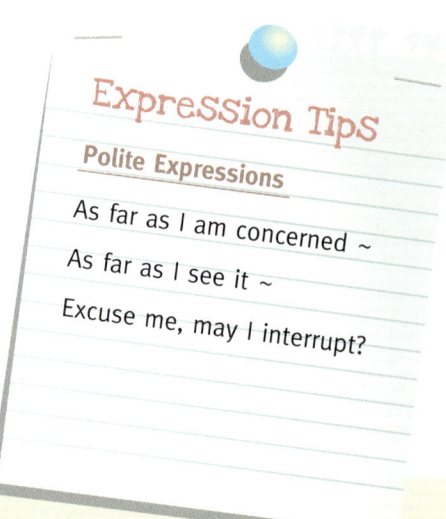

Expression Tips

Polite Expressions

As far as I am concerned ~
As far as I see it ~
Excuse me, may I interrupt?

Time to Debate

Choose one statement. Debate the statement in groups.
(One group agrees with the statement, the other group disagree with the statement.)

1. It's better to be home-schooled.
2. Cooperation can help us solve the world's problems.
3. School is too competitive.

UNIT 5 Cosmetic Surgery

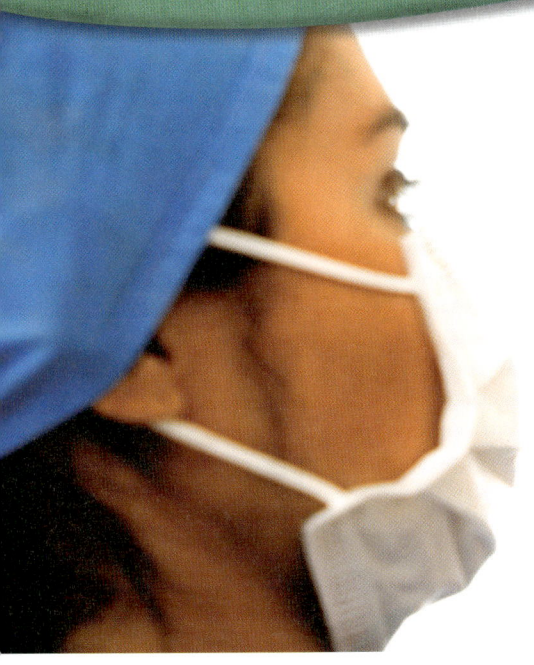
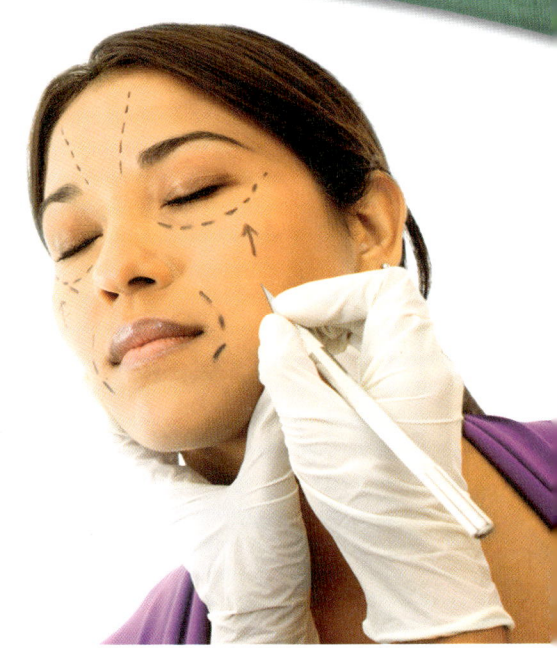

Warm-up

- **If you could change yourself, how would you change?**

Brain	
Skeleton	
Arms and Legs	
Heart and lungs	
Stomach	
Eyes	

- **Interview your classmates using the questions below.**

   1. What part of your body are you happy with?
   2. What part of your body are you unhappy with?

Cosmetic Surgery

🔸 **Read the passage.**

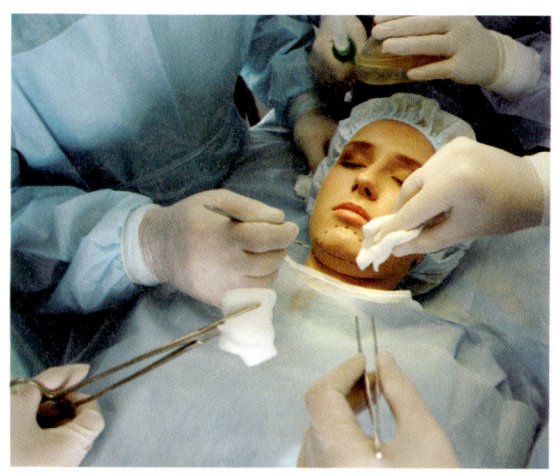

Some people believe that image is very important. For those people, how we look is who we are. In 2009 in the United States, 11 million cosmetic surgery operations were done. Cosmetic surgery is a very big business. In Europe, people paid more than 2.2 billion dollars for cosmetic surgery operations.

There are many popular types of cosmetic surgery. Nose jobs and tummy tucks are popular in the west. Eyelid surgery is popular in the east. If you can afford it, it is easy to change your appearance. Cosmetic surgery operations are often very short operations and the patient often recovers quickly. Some people say they are more confident with their new appearances. They say we are free to do what we like with our bodies. However, accidents do happen and sometimes people look strange or ugly after their surgery.

Some people also become addicted to cosmetic surgery. They continue to have more and more surgeries because they want to look perfect. This can cause a kind of mental illness.

Cosmetic surgery is popular, partly because of the media. When we watch movies and television we see people who have had many cosmetic surgeries. We think these people are perfect and we feel inferior to them. Often the pictures of models in magazines are computer generated and it is not possible to look that way. That does not stop people from trying.

Comprehension Check — Answer the questions.

1. What are some popular types of cosmetic surgery?
2. Where is eyelid surgery popular?
3. How many cosmetic surgeries were performed in the United States in 2009?
4. What are the dangers of plastic surgery?
5. Why do some say plastic surgery is popular?

Vocabulary Check — Complete the sentence with a word from the box.

cosmetics	recover	mental	media	inferior

1. Your _____ health is as important as having a healthy body.
2. You shouldn't feel _____ to those people because you're as smart as they are.
3. After your surgery, it will take time to _____.
4. I wanted to look better, so I had put on _____.
5. The scandal was widely reported in the _____.

Think About It

Think about the advantages and disadvantages of cosmetic surgery.

Advantages
- Can enhance self confidence
-
-

Disadvantages
- Promotes the idea that image is everything
-
-

Opinion Practice

- **Practice supporting/refuting the opinions.**

   Supporting Opinions

   1. People should be allowed to have plastic surgery... _____
   2. Plastic surgery is too dangerous... _____
   3. Plastic surgery makes you more confident... _____
   4. The media is responsible for making plastic surgery popular... _____

   > a. because you are happier with your body.
   > b. because it is their body and their choice.
   > c. because people can become addicted and mistakes happen.
   > d. because every day we see beautiful people on TV and magazines.

   Refuting Opinions

   1. Your appearance is the most important thing about you. _____
   2. The only way to gain confidence is with plastic surgery. _____
   3. People will only like me if I have plastic surgery. _____
   4. Plastic surgery is the fastest and safest way to change your appearance. _____

   > a. People will like you because you are nice and a good person, not because of how you look.
   > b. Yes, it is fast, but plastic surgery is very dangerous and mistakes do happen.
   > c. It is possible to gain confidence by going on a diet, working hard or trying new things.
   > d. This is not true. It is more important to be nice to people than to look better than them.

Opinion Examples

- Read the opinions and answer the questions.

Opinion A

Track 14

❝ Some people see the benefits of plastic surgery. Others see disadvantages. Basically, it is a personal decision. If we have enough money, we are each free to choose how we look. If I decide to get a nose job, I am the one who is most affected. It does not harm others. For this reason, if I want to gain self confidence by changing my appearance, it is a personal matter. I should be free to make any decision I like. ❞

Opinion B

Track 15

❝ I think that people who get plastic surgery are superficial. When I look in the mirror, I know that my appearance is not perfect. Maybe my ears could be a little smaller or forehead a little less wrinkly. So what? It's not so important how I look. I think a person is defined by their actions and their words, not by their appearance. It is always important to dress appropriately and neatly. However, I don't think we should judge people by their appearance. ❞

1. Please circle the main idea in each opinion.

2. Please underline the supporting ideas in each opinion.

3. What could you further say to support the opinion with which you agree?

Discussion Questions

● **Discuss the questions in groups.**

1. Do you know anyone who's had cosmetic surgery? Please tell your group about it.

2. Would you ever consider using surgery to change your appearance? Please explain your answer.

3. How does your appearance affect your life? How would your life be different if you were extremely beautiful? Extremely ugly?

4. Are attractive people treated differently? How so?

5. Which do you think is more important; how a person looks or how a person acts? Why?

Expression Tips
Polite Expressions
I think ~
I would say that ~
I'm afraid I don't agree.

Time to Debate

Choose one statement. Debate the statement in groups.
(One group agrees with the statement, the other group disagree with the statement..)

1. Image is everything.

2. Cosmetic surgery increases self confidence.

3. Only vain people get cosmetic surgery.

UNIT 6 Family

ED1-06
MP3

Warm-up

- Fill in the family tree with celebrity names. Who is your father? Is your mother a politician or a movie star?

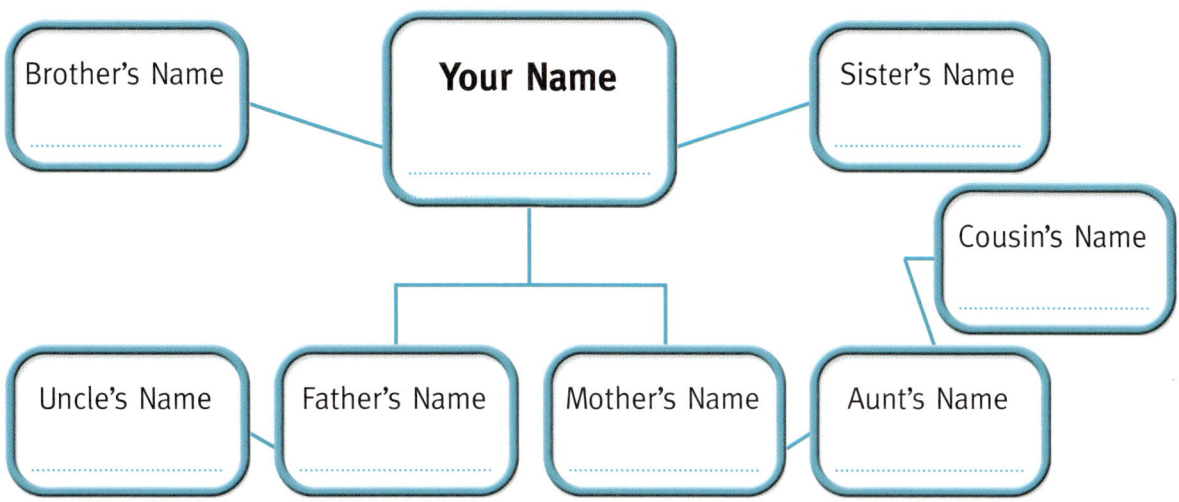

- Interview a classmate using the questions below - they should be about your real family, not the family you made up above.

  1. Are you the youngest or oldest in your family?
  2. How many cousins do you have?

Family

○ **Read the passage.**

Our first relationships in life are with family. Our parents and siblings are our first friends and our first teachers. As we grow up, we still cherish those relationships. However, families today are very different from families in the past.

In the past it was more common for families to have many children. The average American family had 8 children in the year 1800. Now the average family has only 2 children. What is the reason for this change? It may be because many women no longer stay at home to raise children. If they have careers outside the home, they may wish to keep their jobs rather than stay home. Many women are waiting until they are older to have a child, and then may choose to have only one. Now it's not unusual to be an only child.

Other countries have also followed the trend toward smaller families. Sociologists say it happened as they became wealthier. In areas affected by poverty, having more children is seen as a benefit. Children can earn extra money for the family. In richer places, people have greater access to birth control. It's easier for them to plan a smaller family.

Growing up with many siblings teaches a child how to relate to people. Many children can also help with the home or the family business. Then again, parents with many children don't have as much time for each one. Being an only child means you have your parents' undivided attention. They also have more money to spend on you. However, you don't have siblings to play with.

Comprehension Check   Answer the questions.

1. What was the average number of children for American families in 1800?
2. What is the average number of children in an American family now?
3. When did other countries start having smaller families?
4. How does poverty affect family size?
5. What is changing in women's lives?

Vocabulary Check   Complete each sentence with a word or words from the box.

| cherish | average | trends | sociologists | relate |

1. I _____ the memory of my grandparents.
2. The _____ grade on the test was C.
3. _____ say that people need to have strong communities.
4. Playing sports helped me learn to _____ to other kids.
5. The latest _____ in fashion can be found in magazines.

Think About It

1. Think about the advantages and disadvantages of a large family.

Advantages of a large family
- Family members are never alone.
-
-

Disadvantages of a large family
- Less attention for each child
-
-

2. Think about the advantages and disadvantages of a small family.

Advantages of a small family
- More attention for each child
-
-

Disadvantages of a small family
- Only children may be spoiled or bored.
-
-

Opinion Practice

● **Practice supporting/refuting the opinions.**

Supporting Opinions

1. Families today should be small... _____
2. Children should have many brothers and sisters... _____
3. It is better to be an only child... _____
4. Families that need money should have many children... _____

> a. because you will get all of your parents' attention.
>
> b. because the population of the world is becoming too big.
>
> c. because the children can bring more money into the family.
>
> d. so that they will have more people to play with and to learn from in the family.

Refuting Opinions

1. Being an only child is better than having brothers and sisters. _____
2. Parents should make all of their children work at a young age. _____
3. You should compete with your siblings to be the best. _____
4. Your family is more important than your friends. _____

> a. It is the responsibility of parents to give their young children a good education before they begin to work.
>
> b. This is not true for every person. It is good to have brothers and sisters because you can learn many things from them and play with them.
>
> c. Yes, but your friends are important, too. You spend a lot of time with your friends and learn many things from them.
>
> d. No, you should cooperate with your siblings and live happily together.

Opinion Examples

Read the opinions and answer the questions.

Track 17

❝ I think a bigger family is best. If I had more brothers and sisters, I'd have more people to have fun with. There would always be someone to play with me, and we'd all keep each other company. We would divide up all the chores, so work would seem easy. We'd learn from each other, too. All the older kids would teach the younger ones how to read and write. If you don't have brothers and sisters, you don't really learn how to relate to people. A family prepares you for life, so the more the merrier! ❞

Opinion B

Track 18

❝ I believe that a smaller family is better. It's difficult to share your parents with a lot of brothers and sisters. When would they have time for you? Also, if you had many brothers and sisters, you would have to babysit them all the time. That wouldn't leave much time for having fun. Kids should be able to do normal, fun things. If they have too many responsibilities, they can't. One or two kids are just the right amount. That way, a child gets the proper amount of time and attention. ❞

1. Please circle the main idea in each opinion.

2. Please underline the supporting ideas in each opinion.

3. What could you say to further support the opinion with which you agree?

Discussion Questions

● **Discuss the questions in groups.**

1. What do you think of the change from larger to smaller families? Support your opinion.

2. Do you think children from large families have an advantage or a disadvantage? Explain your answer.

3. How does family size affect the way family members relate to each other? Support your opinion.

4. How does family size affect a family's finances? Support your opinion.

5. Do you think the trend will ever go back to larger families? Support your opinion.

Expression Tips

Polite Expressions

In my opinion ~

Is it okay if I interrupt?

It seems to me that ~

Time to Debate

Choose one statement. Debate the statement in groups.
(One group agrees with the statement, the other group disagree with the statement.)

1. It's better to have big families.

2. Children from small families are more likely to be successful.

3. Having large families is foolish and irresponsible.

UNIT 7 Pets

ED1-07
MP3

Warm-up

- Pick the best aspects of different pets and draw a perfect pet for yourself. What will it look like? A cat-turtle-dog? A parrot-lizard-cat?

| |
| |

Why will it be the perfect pet?

- Interview a classmate using the questions below.

  1. If you could have any kind of pet, what would it be? Why?
  2. Do you prefer cats or dogs? Why?

Pets

○ **Read the passage.**

In the United States, about 63% of people have a pet of some sort. It is estimated that owning a dog will cost almost $30,000 over the dog's whole life. Owning pets like cats and dogs is also becoming popular in other parts of the world. Other types of animals also make popular pets. Birds are kept for their beautiful songs. Fish make good pets because they are cheap and easy to care for. It is clear that many people are willing to spend a great deal of time and money to keep animals in their homes. They perceive many benefits from these pets.

First, many believe that pets provide unconditional love. Pets are always happy to see their owners and do not judge them. Pets provide companionship for us and keep us from feeling lonely. There is also evidence that having a pet can improve your health. Pet-owners have a lower risk of a heart attack.

However, there is a problem with pet overpopulation. In the US, more than three million dogs and cats are euthanized each year. People purchase cats and dogs but sometimes get tired of the responsibility and put their pets out on the street. These pets become a nuisance.

It seems that there are many benefits to having pets. However, pet owners must be willing to care for their pets for their entire lives. They must be ready to pay the bills and clean up after their pets. If they can do those things, they'll enjoy all the benefits that go along with the responsibility.

Comprehension Check Answer the questions.

1. Why do people keep birds or fish?
2. What health benefits do pet owners experience?
3. What happens when people get tired of their responsibilities to their pets?
4. What kind of love do pets provide to their owners?
5. How many dogs and cats are euthanized in the US every year?

Vocabulary Check Complete each sentence with a word from the box.

unconditional	judge	companionship	provide	euthanized

1. Children expect _____ love from their parents.
2. Don't _____ me for my lifestyle.
3. The horse was injured and had to be _____.
4. My parents _____ me with food and clothing.
5. I need to have friends and family for _____.

Think About It

Answer the questions.

1. Do pets love their owners as much as their owners love them? Explain.
2. Should pets be allowed in stores and restaurants? Why or why not?
3. If an animal is suffering, should it be euthanized or allowed to live?

Opinion Practice

- **Practice supporting/refuting the opinions.**

Supporting Opinions

1. Fish are great pets... _____
2. Pigs aren't actually dirty... _____
3. Having pets is a great idea... _____
4. It is bad to have an elephant as a pet... _____

   a. because they are too big, and it would be very expensive to feed them.
   b. because they only roll in the dirt and play in mud when they have nowhere else to go.
   c. because they are pretty, cheap and easy to care for.
   d. because they provide companionship and can even improve your health.

Refuting Opinions

1. Cats are smarter than dogs. _____
2. Cats are cheaper than dogs. A cat costs $200; a dog costs $400. _____
3. Cats are cuter than dogs. _____
4. Cats are clean; dogs are very dirty. _____

   a. That's easy to solve. Give your dog a bath!
   b. That's not true. Dogs are smarter than cats. They can learn tricks.
   c. That's not necessarily true! You can often get puppies for free.
   d. That's not always true. Some dogs such as cocker spaniels, are very cute, while some cats are mean and ugly.

Opinion Examples

● **Read the opinions and answer the questions.**

Opinion A

Track 20

❝ I think keeping pets is a waste of money. We live in a world where money is tighter and tighter but still people waste money on keeping expensive pets. Many people in the world are starving, yet millions of dollars are spent on animals every year. Not only is there the food but often there are costly vet bills. Also, many pets are expensive to purchase. Even if you go the pound and get a dog, it will still be expensive, never mind if you get some sort of purebred. In my case, I can find much better ways to spend my money. ❞

Opinion B

Track 21

❝ I think pets teach young children valuable lessons. If a child has a pet, that child learns to take care of another living thing. Pets need to be cared for in a lot of different ways. They need to be groomed and fed on a regular basis. Often, pets need to be trained to live in a house. As children are able to complete these tasks, they learn responsibility and time management skills. Furthermore, pets provide companionship for young children as they grow. It is also important to mention that sometimes it works the other way around and pets look after children! ❞

1. Please circle the main idea in each opinion.
2. Please underline the supporting ideas in each opinion.
3. What could you say to further support the opinion with which you agree?

45

Discussion Questions

● **Discuss the questions in groups.**

1. Do you think it's fair to have large dogs in the city? Why or why not?

2. Are there some pets people should not be allowed to have? What kinds, and why?

3. What should be done about people who don't take proper care of their animals? Support your opinion.

4. Should animals' rights be recognized? Support your opinion.

5. Do you think some people are too extreme in their love for their pets? If so, what kind of behavior is an example?

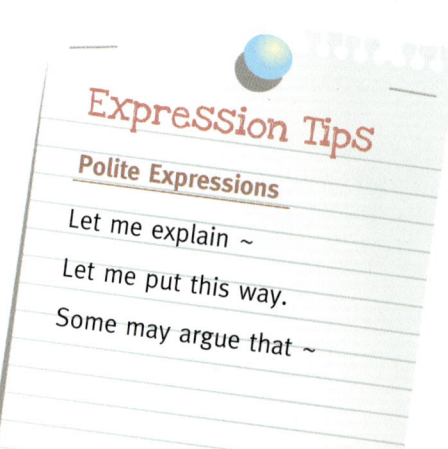

Expression Tips

Polite Expressions

Let me explain ~

Let me put this way.

Some may argue that ~

Time to Debate

Choose one statement. Debate the statement in groups.
(One group agrees with the statement, the other group disagree with the statement.)

1. Animals have feelings just like humans.

2. It's cruel to keep animals in cages.

3. It should be illegal to keep dangerous pets.

UNIT 8 Valentine's Day

Warm-up

● **Match the holidays with their activities.**

Holiday	Halloween
Activity	trick or treat, parade

Holiday	
Activity	

Holiday	
Activity	

● **Interview your classmates using the questions below.**

1. Do you and your friends exchange valentines? What do the cards say?
2. Name 5 gifts people can buy for each other on Valentine's Day.

Valentine's Day

🟠 **Read the passage.**

St. Valentine's Day is a major holiday in many parts of the world. It is celebrated throughout North and South America, Western Europe and parts of Asia. Some view the holiday as a harmless opportunity to celebrate love while others see it as another opportunity to promote consumerism.

February 14th marks the day Valentinus, a Roman priest, was killed in the third century. He helped Christians who were being persecuted by the Roman emperor Claudius. The legend says he even married a few Christian couples. The emperor didn't approve of Christianity. The emperor had him thrown in jail and condemned to death. That's why he's considered the patron saint of couples to this day. How true is this story? No one really knows for sure.

Valentine's Day started being a romantic holiday where people exchange cards and gifts only 150 years ago. Since that time, Valentine's Day has become very popular. For example, more than 190 million valentines are sent in the US every year. Today some of us feel obliged to buy gifts of flowers, chocolate or even jewelry for our loved ones.

Some people call Valentine's Day a 'Hallmark Holiday.' Hallmark is a very large greeting card company in the US. These people suggest that Valentine's is encouraged by companies who only want to sell more goods. Others of us are happy to have a chance to celebrate our relationships by exchanging gifts. Valentine's Day is the perfect time to receive a letter from a secret admirer, or take someone special out on a date.

Comprehension Check — Answer the questions.

1. For whom is Valentine's Day named?
2. What happened to him?
3. What is he the patron saint of?
4. When did Valentine's Day become a romantic holiday?
5. What do some of us feel obliged to do on Valentine's Day?

Vocabulary Check — Complete the sentence with a word from the box.

saint	persecute	consider	obliged	patron

1. It's wrong to _____ people because of their religious beliefs.
2. The _____ spent his life healing the sick and preaching.
3. I don't _____ myself a very good student.
4. They received a large donation from a wealthy _____.
5. Don't feel _____ to help me. I can do it myself.

Think About It

Answer the questions.

1. Do 'Hallmark holidays' like Valentine's Day serve any purpose? Why or why not?

2. Is it better to buy a gift or make a gift for someone you care about? Explain your answer.

3. What would be a good Valentine's Day gift?

Opinion Practice

- **Practice supporting/refuting the opinions.**

   Supporting Opinions

   1. Businesses enjoy Valentine's Day... _____
   2. Valentine's Day should be celebrated... _____
   3. Flowers are good Valentine's Day gifts... _____
   4. You should get your loved one a Valentine's Day gift... _____

   > a. because the gift will show your loved one that you love them.
   >
   > b. because they are beautiful and romantic.
   >
   > c. because it is a nice way to spend time with the people you love.
   >
   > d. because people spend a lot of money on gifts and cards.

   Refuting Opinions

   1. If you do not get a Valentine's Day gift it means no one loves you. _____
   2. Jewelry is a better gift then flowers. _____
   3. You must buy all of your friends a gift for Valentine's Day. _____
   4. Only very expensive gifts are romantic. _____

   > a. You do not need to spend a lot of money to be romantic. You can even make your own gift!
   >
   > b. That is not true. Many people do not celebrate Valentine's Day, and they still might love you.
   >
   > c. No, you should only buy gifts for very special people like a boyfriend or girlfriend.
   >
   > d. No way! Jewelry is too expensive, and flowers are very beautiful.

Opinion Examples

Read the opinions and answer the questions.

Track 23

Valentine's Day is an opportunity to show your boyfriend or girlfriend how much you love them. In the days before Valentine's Day, you can see flowers and candy in every store window. That makes it easy to remember to buy a gift. Valentine's Day also makes it easy to know how they feel about you. If they bring you large presents, they love you a great deal. I always look forward to Valentine's Day. I love flowers and candy, and I also like to know how much I'm loved.

Opinion B

Track 24

Valentine's Day is an example of corporations trying to tell me what to do and when to do it. If I would like to bring some flowers or candy to someone, I can do so anytime of the year. If I don't bring home some flowers and chocolates on Valentine's Day, I am seen as cold-hearted. I don't think that's fair. Wouldn't it be better to bring someone chocolates on another day? That way, they would know that I didn't have to, but wanted to give a present.

1. Please circle the main idea in each opinion.

2. Please underline the supporting ideas in each opinion.

3. What more could you say to support the opinion with which you agree?

Discussion Questions

● **Discuss the questions in groups.**

1. What do you think about 'Hallmark holidays?' Do they take advantage of people's feelings of guilt or insecurity? Why or why not?

2. What do you think about the kinds of gifts that are popular on Valentine's Day? Are there any that you would like to receive? Why or why not?

3. Do you think Valentinus did the right thing to marry Christian couples even though it was illegal? Why or why not?

4. Is giving a valentine a real sign of love and affection? Why or why not?

5. Could Valentine's Day be depressing for some people? Why or why not?

Expression Tips

Polite Expressions

Some people say that ~

Thank you for pointing that out.

The way I see it ~

Choose one statement. Debate the statement in groups.
(One group agrees with the statement, the other group disagrees with the statement.)

1. Valentine's Day is a silly and meaningless holiday.

2. It's a good idea to have a day where people can express their feelings.

3. You can tell how much you are loved by the number of valentines you receive.

Internet Anonymity

Warm-up

● 1. Create your own invention with a two-word name.
   (Example: lion + tiger = liger, internet + notebook = netbook)

> It is called, _____

2. Answer the following questions and check them with your teacher.

> - What does it do?
> - Who uses it?
> - Why would to be a good idea for a company to make this product?

● Interview your classmates using the questions below.

1. What are some internet activities that allow anonymous participation?
2. Do people communicate differently when they're anonymous? How?

53

Internet Anonymity

Read the passage.

Internet anonymity is a very complex issue. It involves ideas about responsibility, community and freedom of speech. It is important to note that the internet is a relatively new method of communication and with that comes new ways of communicating. We act differently if we speak in person, talk to each other on the phone or communicate online.

Currently, we can write anything we like on our blogs, in chat rooms or on message boards, without using our real names. Our words can be anonymous. Some of us want that changed. They think we should attach our names to everything we write or post on the internet. Some of us want things to stay as they are.

Internet anonymity affects a number of different online situations. If we use our names in every situation, it may prevent people from writing mean and hurtful things about others. People might be ashamed to put their name along with such vulgar writing. However, this may also harm our freedom to speak and write. Individuals or groups who have different opinions about government officials and their policies may not feel free to express their opinions. This can harm democracy.

We live in a culture where people watch less television and read fewer newspapers than they did ten years ago. Now, we get our views of the world around us from the internet. Decisions that we make about internet anonymity will affect not only our behavior online but also our freedom.

Comprehension Check Answer the questions.

1. If we had to use our names online, what positive effects could that have?
2. What negative effects could it have?
3. How is our culture different than it was 10 years ago?
4. What makes the issue of internet anonymity complex?
5. What is the state of internet anonymity right now?

Vocabulary Check Complete the sentence with a word from the box.

| anonymous | vulgar | method | communicate | policy |

1. Email and phone are the ways I _____ most often.
2. The complaint came from a(n) _____ phone caller.
3. We were upset to see _____ words written on the wall.
4. I'll show you the best _____ of baking a cake.
5. It's our _____ to refund your money if you return a purchase.

Think About It

Answer the questions.

1. What do you think would happen if we had to sign our names on everything we did online?

2. How do you know what to believe when you read it on the internet?

3. Do your parents monitor your internet use? What are they concerned about?

Opinion Practice

● **Practice supporting/refuting the opinions.**

Supporting Opinions

1. People should be forced to use their real name on the internet... _____
2. Internet anonymity is too dangerous... _____
3. Being anonymous on the internet is good... _____
4. Everyone should be given free speech... _____

> a. because people are more likely to do bad things if they believe no one will know who they are.
>
> b. because it will make people be more responsible for their actions.
>
> c. because you can hide information about yourself from other people.
>
> d. because we should be allowed to say what we believe.

Refuting Opinions

1. Free speech is the most important thing we have in society. _____
2. We should ban the internet because it is not safe. _____
3. Sometimes it is too embarrassing to use you real name on the internet. _____
4. You should be allowed to protect your privacy on the internet. _____

> a. No, the internet is a public place so everyone should be allowed to see your personal information.
>
> b. That is a bad solution. The internet is too important to ban. We can try and make it safer.
>
> c. That is silly. You should never be embarrassed about the things that you do.
>
> d. It is important to be able to say what we believe, but it is more important to be safe and free from danger.

Opinion Examples

- **Read the opinions and answer the questions.**

Opinion A

Track 26

❝ I think that many problems would be solved if people were forced to use their real names on the internet. People would be less likely to use vulgar language and say rude things. When people are anonymous, they feel like it's ok to be cruel. They say things they would never say in person. When this kind of behavior is widespread, it lowers our standards. Then we think it's normal to be rude. The more responsibility we have for our behavior, the better we behave. We should always be willing to attach our name to our words. ❞

Opinion B

Track 27

❝ Many countries guarantee freedom of speech and freedom of the press. We might not write our ideas if we had to include our names. Especially if we had different opinions than the government or if our ideas were unpopular. We would be afraid of punishment. However, that's what freedom of speech is - the freedom to speak your mind without fear of punishment. If we abandon internet anonymity, we will lose our freedom of speech. This freedom is an important part of a democracy. ❞

1. Please circle the main idea in each opinion.
2. Please underline the supporting ideas in each opinion.
3. What could you say to further support the opinion with which you agree?

Discussion Questions

● **Discuss the questions in groups.**

1. Do you think freedom of speech gives us the right to say anything? Please support your answer.

2. Why do you think people write hurtful things on the internet that they would never say in person? Please explain.

3. In Opinion A, it says "We should always be willing to attach our name to our words." Why should we?

4. Should people feel responsible for each other's feelings, even if they don't know each other? Why or why not?

5. Have you ever read something online that upset you? Was it anonymous? What was it?

Expression Tips
Active Expressions
I insist (that) ~
I'm confident (that) ~
I'm sure (that) ~

Choose one statement. Debate the statement in groups.
(One group agrees with the statement, the other group disagree with the statement.)

1. Internet anonymity is the best way to let people say what they really think.

2. People should be required to give their name in some online situations.

3. Protecting internet anonymity is the same as protecting a person.

UNIT 10 Success and Happiness

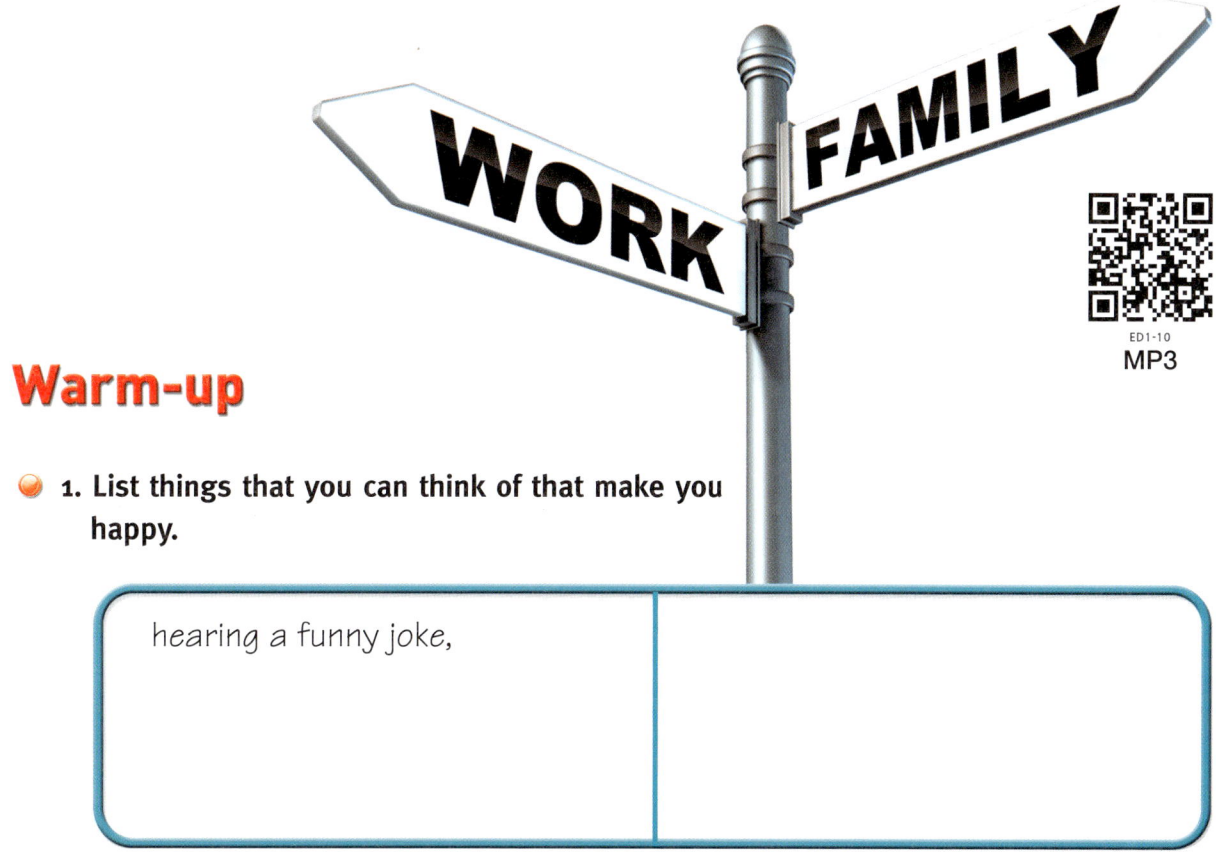

Warm-up

- 1. List things that you can think of that make you happy.

hearing a funny joke,	

- 2. Divide the above list into two columns.

Things that make you happy quickly	Things that make you happy after a while

- Interview your classmates using the questions below.

  1. Who is the most successful person you know? What makes them successful?
  2. What kinds of careers do you think make people successful?

Success and Happiness

● **Read the passage.**

Success and happiness are two very subjective terms. These words have different meanings for each of us. What makes one person happy might make another person miserable and what one person calls a success, another may see as a failure. An artist who completes a sculpture, a scientist working on a formula, and a farmer at harvest time each have different criteria for evaluating success and happiness.

When some people speak of success these days they mean career and wealth. To these people a successful person is usually someone who has sacrificed time, values or happiness to become wealthy and powerful.

When we speak of happiness these days we are usually talking about family and time. When we speak of a happy person, it is usually someone who has the time to spend with friends and family, and do things they feel are useful and enjoyable.

Throughout our lives, we each deal with happiness and success as well as sadness and failure. We make decisions about how we spend our time based on our values. It is important to remember that what is right for one person is not right for everyone, and that we are each responsible for how we spend our time. How will we feel when we are old and look back on our lives? Will we wish we were more wealthy and powerful, or will we wish we were happier?

Comprehension Check — Answer the questions.

1. What do some people mean by 'success?'
2. What things do people sacrifice for this kind of success?
3. What do we usually mean by 'happiness?'
4. How do we make decisions about how we spend our time?
5. How are the terms 'success' and 'happiness' subjective?

Vocabulary Check — Complete the sentence with a word from the box.

term	sacrifice	miserable	evaluated	value

1. I felt _____ after we lost the game.
2. What do you mean by the _____ 'unbelievable?'
3. I _____ hard work and honesty most of all.
4. At the end of the year our work will be _____.
5. I would _____ a week's allowance to have those cool shoes.

Think About It

Answer the questions.

1. Is it possible to be successful and unsuccessful at the same time? Explain.

2. Is anyone happy all the time? How can you tell?

3. Do you think being extremely rich would make you happy? For how long?

Opinion Practice

- **Practice supporting/refuting the opinions.**

Supporting Opinions

1. You should do things you enjoy... _____
2. You should not be afraid to fail... _____
3. Everyone should take time to relax in the day... _____
4. You should never give up... _____

   a. because people who quit when they fail will not become successful.
   b. because working all day can be very stressful.
   c. because it makes you a happier person.
   d. because we learn more from our mistakes than from our successes.

Refuting Opinions

1. If you fail you will never be successful. _____
2. You are only successful if you are rich. _____
3. You should always work hard and never relax. _____
4. Happiness is more important than being a success. _____

   a. This is not true. Thomas Edison failed 1,000 times before he succeeded in inventing the light bulb!
   b. This is a bad idea. Everyone needs time to relax and have fun. If you always work you will be stressed out.
   c. No, it is more important to be a success so you can have a good job and be rich.
   d. There are many different ways to be successful. You can be successful if you get good grades in school.

Opinion Examples

Read the opinions and answer the questions.

Opinion A

Track 29

"It's possible to be happy without being successful. At least, you don't have to be rich to be happy. Many people think that wealth is the same as success. However, recent research shows that rich people are no happier than middle class people. It's true that we need food and shelter. We need enough money to take care of our basic needs. But all the things we buy with extra money don't actually make us happier in the long run. They just make people envy us."

Opinion B

Track 30

"Success and happiness are related things because you cannot have one without the other. It is impossible to be successful and not be happy. If you are a successful doctor, you earn a lot of money and you're well respected among your colleagues, you will be happy. It is also impossible to be happy with failure. If your business fails and you are broke and disgraced, how could you be happy? We should be concerned with success first and then happiness will follow."

1. Please circle the main idea in each opinion.
2. Please underline the supporting ideas in each opinion.
3. What would you say to further support the opinion with which you agree?

Discussion Questions

● **Discuss the questions in groups.**

1. How wealthy do you need to be to be successful?

2. How wealthy do you need to be to be happy?

3. Can a person be successful even if they hurt a lot of people to get there?

4. Can a person be happy if they are always worried about what other people think of them?

5. How important is friendship to happiness? To success? Explain.

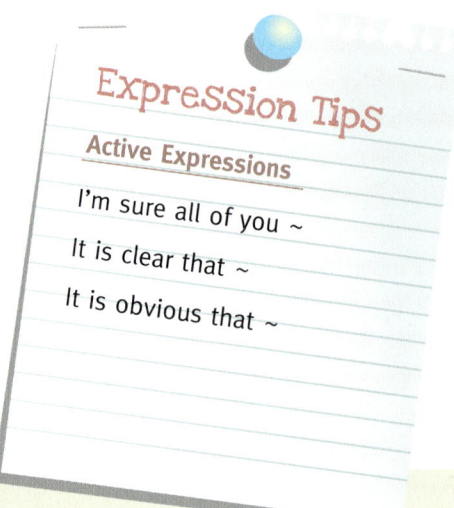

Expression Tips

Active Expressions

I'm sure all of you ~

It is clear that ~

It is obvious that ~

Choose one statement. Debate the statement in groups.
(One group agrees with the statement, the other group disagree with the statement.)

1. You cannot be both successful and happy.

2. Money cannot buy happiness.

3. True success means you've reached your own goals, not society's expectations.

UNIT 11 Pollution

Warm-up

● Find the effect in List B for each cause in List A.

List A	List B
1. power plants that burn coal	a. noise pollution
2. too many bright lights	b. light pollution
3. too many honking horns	c. smog in the sky
4. big farms that use lots of chemicals	d. groundwater pollution
5. aerosol spray cans	e. the hole in the ozone layer

What can we do to make less pollution?

● Interview a classmate using the questions below.

1. Name 3 different causes of pollution.
2. What harm does pollution do? Name 3 kinds.

Pollution

● Read the passage.

Some of us live in a world of convenience. We have cars that take us from place to place, and we heat our houses in the winter and cool them in the summer. Fresh water runs in our houses. Electricity flows and we enjoy goods produced in factories. Though our lives seem convenient, in reality the way we live causes a huge amount of pollution.

There are many different types of pollution. The two major types are air and water pollution. The primary causes of air pollution are emissions from cars and factories. Cars and factories emit many different kinds of chemicals into the air that effect people, animals, plants and the environment in general. Air pollution is responsible for the deaths of more than 600,000 people in China each year.

Water pollution is also a serious worldwide problem. Because of water polluted by factories and poor sanitation, more than 14,000 people a day die. In the spring of 2010, there was a huge oil spill in the Gulf of Mexico. An oil well burst and more than two million liters of oil spilled into the ocean every day for weeks. Water pollution like that has serious effects on fish and coastal animals.

Pollution is the byproduct of our societies. How we deal with creating new pollution and cleaning up already polluted areas in the next generation will be up to each of us.

Comprehension Check Answer the questions.

1. How many people die each day from water pollution?
2. What are the two major types of pollution?
3. What are the primary causes of air pollution?
4. There was an oil spill in the spring of 2010. Where was it?
5. How do we know air pollution is a serious problem in China?

Vocabulary Check Complete the sentence with a word from the box.

emissions	sanitation	byproducts	spill	burst

1. Many of the _____ created in our factory must be thrown out.
2. Newer cars make less _____ and are better for the environment.
3. If you're not careful with your drink, you may have a(n) _____.
4. I accidentally _____ my balloon.
5. Restaurants must be careful about _____ to ensure food safety.

Think About It

Answer the questions.

1. Many say pollution is our most serious problem. Do you agree? Why or why not?

2. How is your life affected by pollution?

3. Can young people make a difference in the fight against pollution?

Opinion Practice

● **Practice supporting/refuting the opinions.**

Supporting Opinions

1. You should study about pollution and think of ways to stop it... _____
2. Everyone should recycle paper... _____
3. Smoking should be banned everywhere... _____
4. You should turn the lights off when you leave the house... _____

> a. because it will save electricity.
> b. because it is bad for the environment and bad for your health.
> c. because we will have to cut down less trees.
> d. because having a clean planet is important for our future.

Refuting Opinions

1. Cars produce too much air pollution. We should stop using cars. _____
2. My life is not affected by pollution, so why should I care? _____
3. Children are too young to help stop pollution. _____
4. Air pollution is more serious than water pollution. _____

> a. They are both serious because we cannot live without clean air and water.
> b. That is not a practical solution. We need cars to work and travel. We can make more energy efficient cars.
> c. That's not true. Everyone is affected by pollution because we share this planet. If it is polluted everyone will suffer.
> d. You are never too young to help. Children can influence their parents to recycle more.

Opinion Examples

- Read the opinions and answer the questions.

Opinion A

Track 32

❝ These days, many people are talking about the problem of pollution. Everyone is upset about polluted water and dirty air. However, we are not ready to completely change our lifestyles. Let's face it. Technology allows us to enjoy so many benefits. Convenience and comfort have made our lives better. We would have to let go of so many wonderful things to change this problem of pollution. Maybe it's better to just accept it: pollution is the price of our convenient lives. It seems like a price we are willing to pay. ❞

Opinion B

Track 33

❝ Pollution is a serious problem. But I have a three step solution: Reduce, Reuse and Recycle! We need to use less water and energy, and not buy stuff that we don't need. We also need to drive our cars less often. We need to reuse things instead of throwing them in the garbage. Lastly, we need to recycle paper, metal, plastic and glass. If everyone follows these three easy steps there will be a lot less pollution. Are you ready to reduce, reuse and recycle? ❞

1. Please circle the main idea in each opinion.

2. Please underline the supporting ideas in each opinion.

3. What could you say to further support the opinion with which you agree?

Discussion Questions

● **Discuss the questions in groups.**

1. Do you think most people take environmental problems seriously enough? Explain your answer.

2. What kinds of lifestyle changes will we have to make to save the environment? Is it worth it?

3. A lot of advertising talks about going 'green'. How much of this advertising is genuine, and how much is just following the trend?

4. Who should be responsible for taking care of the environment? Should it be the government? The factories? Or us, the consumers? Explain your answer.

5. Some people say it's too expensive to become environmentally friendly. They say it will hurt the economy too much. Do you agree with this? Why or why not?

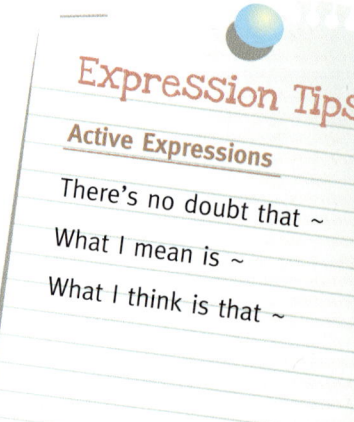

Expression Tips
Active Expressions
There's no doubt that ~
What I mean is ~
What I think is that ~

Time to Debate

Choose one statement. Debate the statement in groups.
(One group agrees with the statement, the other group disagrees with the statement.)

1. Environmentalists exaggerate the problem. Throughout history, there has always been someone saying the world is about to end. This is no different.

2. We should all stop driving cars, except when absolutely necessary.

3. Our actions now will decide what kind of world our grandchildren will live in.

UNIT 12 Peer Pressure

ED1-12
MP3

Warm-up

- Fill in the table.

Good things that friends might pressure you to do	Bad things that friends might pressure you to do
study	cheat

- **Interview a classmate using the questions below.**

    1. If your friend offered you a cigarette, would you smoke it? Why or why not?
    2. Look at your friends in the class. What is one item of clothing that is very popular?

Peer Pressure

🟠 **Read the passage.**

Track 34

Everyone is a part of many different groups. We are members of families, classes, teams and clubs. We each fit in some places and not in others. Have you ever wanted to be part of a group that did not want you?

Often when you are in a group, there is pressure to do certain things or act in a certain way. This is called 'peer pressure.' It's when your friends want you to think or act like they think and act. Sometimes this is a good thing, sometimes it's bad. For example, you may be in a study group where everyone encourages everyone to study hard and get good grades, and that's a good thing. However, some may be in groups where they are encouraged to steal or to smoke. That's an example of the negative side of peer pressure.

In the 1970's a scientist at Stanford University did a study on peer pressure. He selected 24 students and randomly chose 12 to pretend to be prison guards and 12 to pretend to be prisoners. Within a few short days, the students pretending to be prison guards became mean and violent towards the students pretending to be prisoners. They did things to their classmates that they would never usually do, like make them sleep without beds and blankets or take their food away. This is a terrible example of peer pressure where the guards all encouraged each other to be mean to the prisoners. It is important to remember that we are each responsible for our own actions no matter what group we're in.

Comprehension Check Answer the questions.

1. What is pressure from a group of friends called?
2. What are two examples of negative peer pressure?
3. What university had a study on peer pressure in the 1970s?
4. How many students were selected for the study?
5. What happened in that study?

Vocabulary Check Complete the sentence with a word from the box.

| pressure | peers | randomly | prison | mean |

1. We chose names _____ to decide who would play the game first.
2. The burglars had to pay a huge fine or spend time in _____.
3. It's inappropriate to be _____ to your classmates.
4. Her parents put a lot of _____ on her to succeed at school.
5. At school, you learn to relate to your _____.

Think About It

Answer the questions.

1. Do humans know what's right and wrong when they're born, or must they learn it? Explain your answer.

2. Do we put pressure on other people without realizing it? How?

3. Imagine your friend has been pressured into doing something wrong. What's the best way to tell him or her you don't approve?

Opinion Practice

- **Practice supporting/refuting the opinions.**

Supporting Opinions

1. You should never steal… _____
2. You should never give in to bad peer pressure… _____
3. It is difficult to say no to a friend… _____
4. You should not smoke… _____

> a. because cigarettes are bad for you.
>
> b. because being yourself is more important.
>
> c. because everyone wants their friends to like them and think they are cool.
>
> d. because taking things that don't belong to you is wrong. If you want it you must pay for it.

Refuting Opinions

1. You should always try to fit in with a group. _____
2. You should smoke. It's cool! _____
3. You are weak if you follow peer pressure. _____
4. It is more important to listen to your friends than to listen to your parents. _____

> a. No, it is not cool. Smoking is bad for your health.
>
> b. That is not necessarily true. Strong people use positive peer pressure to help each other succeed.
>
> c. That is not true. You should always listen to your parents because they have much experience and know what is correct.
>
> d. Not always. It is more important to be yourself. Eventually you will find a group that is good for you.

Opinion Examples

- Read the opinions and answer the questions.

Opinion A

Track 35

❝ I am part of a study group that is full of very hard-working students. We meet three times a week and help each other study. To be a part of the group, you need to have an 'A' average. If your grades fall below an 'A' you can't come to the group anymore. Sometimes, we have to kick students out of the group. We all encourage, help and put pressure on each other. Pressure helps us to do better. ❞

Opinion B

Track 36

❝ Peer pressure can be a very dangerous thing. We can be pressured to do things that we would never normally do because of pressure from a group. In the case of war, people are pressured and convinced to kill other people. Normally, most of us would never kill another person. Less extreme is smoking. Often teenagers smoke to look cool so that they can be part of a group. Peer pressure can convince us to do things that are sometimes bad for us. ❞

1. Please circle the main idea in each opinion.

2. Please underline the supporting ideas in each opinion.

3. What could you say to further support the opinion with which you agree?

Discussion Questions

🟠 **Discuss the questions in groups.**

1. Where do you draw the line with peer pressure? Are there things you might agree to do? Are there things you would never do?

2. Do your parents ever warn you about peer pressure? What do they say?

3. What kind of personality type is most affected by peer pressure? What type is the least?

4. Adults may tell you that friends who pressure you are no friends at all. They may say you should ignore them. Is this realistic? Explain.

5. Why do people in groups want to behave similarly?

Expression Tips
Informative Expressions
According to an expert ~
As you can see ~
As you've mentioned ~
Consequently ~

Choose one statement. Debate the statement in groups.
(One group agrees with the statement, the other group disagrees with the statement.)

1. Giving in to peer pressure is a sign of weakness. If you do it when you're young, you'll probably always be weak.

2. Peer pressure can have a positive influence on our lives.

3. If you're pressured to do something bad, it's not all your fault.

UNIT 13 Children Studying Abroad

ED1-13
MP3

Warm-up

- Write the names of countries where you could or might want to study abroad. Write things that could be different about studying in those countries in the spaces below.

Country	Reason to study abroad
USA	learn American English

- Interview a classmate using the questions below.

  1. If you were to study in any other country, which one would you choose? Why?
  2. What can you learn, besides English, studying abroad?

Children Studying Abroad

○ **Read the passage.**

Track 37

Everyone knows that education is a top priority in many Asian countries. It is also true that in many non-English speaking countries, learning English is considered an important part of a complete education. Fluency in English is considered a prerequisite for success. For this reason, many non-native English speakers study abroad. It is not unusual for a student to spend a year or two attending high school or university in an English-speaking country.

Education and English education are becoming more important to parents. As a result, many parents are sending their very young children to study abroad. These days, many elementary school students are leaving their home countries to study in English-speaking countries.

The advantage of studying abroad at a young age is learning English. However, there are many drawbacks. Studying abroad means leaving one or both of your parents behind, and it also means learning a different culture. When you return to your home country it may seem like a foreign place but really, it is your home.

There is a central question to this situation, "Is it worth it?" Is it worth the cost? It costs families a lot of their income to send their children abroad to study. Is it worth the loneliness? Both the child and family will miss each other.

Lastly, all cultures depend on language. Therefore, the non-English speaking countries' cultures depend on their languages. If English has become so important all over the world, what does that say about the importance of other cultures?

Comprehension Check Answer the questions.

1. What is considered a prerequisite for success in many Asian countries?
2. What is the advantage of studying abroad at a young age?
3. What are the drawbacks of studying abroad?
4. How much does it cost families to send their children abroad to study?
5. What do cultures depend on?

Vocabulary Check Complete the sentence with a word from the box.

priority	considered	fluency	prerequisite	drawbacks

1. With a lot of work, I will achieve total _____ in Spanish.
2. Is high school algebra a _____ for university level math?
3. There are benefits to saving all your money, but there are also _____.
4. It's _____ impolite to talk on your cell phone at dinner.
5. You have to make homework a top _____ if you want a good grade.

Think About It

Think about the advantages and disadvantages of studying abroad at a young age.

Advantages
- Learn excellent English
-
-

Disadvantages
- Miss family
-
-

79

Opinion Practice

● **Practice supporting/refuting the opinions.**

Supporting Opinions

1. If you want to learn a new language you should study abroad... _____
2. You should never forget your native language... _____
3. You should call your family often when abroad... _____
4. You need to be strong to study abroad... _____

> a. because your culture depends on your language.
> b. because it will help to keep your relationship strong.
> c. since you will have to use the language everyday in reading, writing, speaking and listening.
> d. because you will face new challenges and will have to be independent.

Refuting Opinions

1. Studying abroad is dangerous. _____
2. If you leave your country you will lose your culture. _____
3. You should stay home because your family will miss you a lot. _____
4. If you study abroad you will get a better job. _____

> a. That's not necessarily true. If you study abroad but do not work hard it will be difficult to get a job.
> b. That's not true. Most people who study abroad are safe and have a very great experience.
> c. Your family might miss you, but modern technology has made it very easy to talk to your family.
> d. No you won't. You can keep your culture and still experience a new one.

Opinion Examples

- **Read the opinions and answer the questions.**

Opinion A

Track 38

❝ I want to have every advantage in my education. If that means going to a foreign country, then I will do it. I realize that it is scary and that I will miss my family, but my education must be the best. If I get an excellent education, then I will score well on my college entrance exams. Then I can get into a good college and get a job where I make a lot of money. I realize it is going to be difficult, but it's really worth it. ❞

Opinion B

Track 39

❝ I wouldn't want to study abroad. I would rather be at home with my friends. I don't think it would feel very good to be shipped off across the ocean where you don't know anyone. Those kids must be very lonely. It would be like going to a new school, except a hundred times worse. If I want to learn English, I can do it here. Some things are not worth the trouble. Studying abroad is one of them. ❞

1. Please circle the main idea in each opinion.

2. Please underline the supporting ideas in each opinion.

3. What could you say to further support the opinion with which you agree?

Discussion Questions

● **Discuss the questions in groups.**

1. How important is keeping your own culture?

2. How does studying abroad affect family relationships?

3. Is studying abroad more stressful than studying in your home country? Why or why not?

4. Does studying abroad give people real advantages? If so, does that mean those who can afford it have an unfair advantage?

5. Can studying abroad have positive effects for your home country?

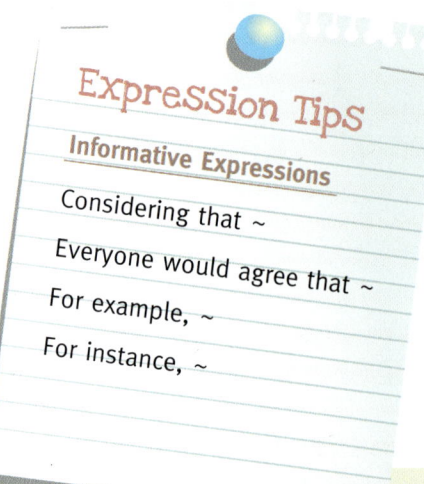

Expression Tips
Informative Expressions
Considering that ~
Everyone would agree that ~
For example, ~
For instance, ~

Choose one statement. Debate the statement in groups.
(One group agrees with the statement, the other group disagrees with the statement.)

1. Studying abroad is the greatest experience you will ever have.

2. Studying abroad is damaging our culture.

3. Your success depends on your dedication, not going abroad.

Unit 14 Corporal Punishment

ED1-14
MP3

Warm-up

● Write what you think would be an appropriate response to the following situations.

Incident	Response
Student is late.	give student a warning
Student threatens teacher.	
Student is openly rude to the teacher - uses bad language when talking to them.	
Student forgets their homework.	
Student cheats on their exam.	
Student gets into a fight with another student.	

● Interview a classmate using the questions below.

1. What are three ways of punishing students in school?
2. What are 2 ways to correct behavior, other than punishment?

83

Corporal Punishment

🟠 **Read the passage.**

Track 40

If we misbehave in school, there are many types of punishment. We might receive a lower grade, or be kept after class. We also might be punished by being given more school work. There are also punishments that cause physical pain and these are called corporal punishment.

Corporal punishment can take many forms. In schools, it usually means being hit with a stick. Many countries around the world have banned corporal punishment in schools but it is still used in some countries. Students are routinely beaten for speaking out of turn, not completing their homework or getting a low score on an exam. Some teachers think this is an effective way of changing students' behavior. For them, corporal punishment saves time, increases the teacher's authority and sends a clear message to the other students in the classroom.

At home, parents may use corporal punishment to discipline their children. They may 'spank' the child. In North America, this has become less popular. More parents are choosing to give consequences that fit the behavior of the child. They may be sent to their room for a 'time out,' or they may be denied some special privilege.

Some parents and teachers disagree with corporal punishment. They believe that violence does not make children behave better. Studies show that corporal punishment increases violent behavior, and that students who receive corporal punishment have lower test scores.

Comprehension Check Answer the questions.

1. What other consequences can parents give, besides corporal punishment?
2. What does corporal punishment usually mean in schools?
3. Why do teachers think corporal punishment is effective?
4. Why might students in some countries receive corporal punishment?
5. What other kinds of punishment can you receive in school?

Vocabulary Check Complete the sentence with a word from the box.

routinely	effective	corporal	ban	authority

1. Exercise is a(n) _____ way of losing weight.
2. A school may _____ certain books if they're too controversial.
3. It's important to respect the _____ of your parents and teachers.
4. We bring our car in for maintenance _____.
5. Of all the punishments available, the _____ kind is the toughest.

Think About It

Answer the questions.

1. What sort of behavior, if any, should result in corporal punishment? Explain.

2. What would you rather receive - corporal punishment or a very difficult assignment?

3. Whom do you respect more - a teacher who uses corporal punishment or a teacher who doesn't? Explain your choice.

Opinion Practice

● **Practice supporting/refuting the opinions.**

Supporting Opinions

1. Corporal punishment should be banned in schools... _____
2. Children should always respect their parents... _____
3. Teachers should be allowed to hit bad students... _____
4. Parents should never hit a child... _____

> a. because the parents will be teaching their children that violence is OK.
>
> b. because correcting students with violence sets a bad example and can make the student hate the teacher.
>
> c. because parents love their children and provide them with the things they need to be successful.
>
> d. because bad children make teaching difficult and they disrupt the class.

Refuting Opinions

1. Strong people use corporal punishment, weak people do not. _____
2. Corporal punishment is the most effective way to discipline children. _____
3. You should be afraid of your teachers. _____
4. You should do your homework so that you will not get in trouble. _____

> a. This is a bad idea. Students should respect their teachers, but they should not be afraid of them. Fear makes learning less fun.
>
> b. You should do your homework because it will prepare you for the future, not because you are afraid of getting in trouble.
>
> c. No it is not. Corporal punishment has been shown to make children do worse in school and can lead to more violence.
>
> d. This is not true. It takes courage to solve a problem without using violence.

Opinion Examples

● **Read the opinions and answer the questions.**

Opinion A

Track 41

❞ Some kids are very bad. They scare the rest of us, and they don't listen to teachers. Sometimes the only way to correct them is with a serious punishment. It's too bad if that hurts them. However, they have had a lot of chances. They just don't listen. They need corporal punishment because no other method has any effect on them. It's really for the good of the whole school. The whole group is better off if bad behavior is stopped. ❞

Opinion B

Track 42

❞ Corporal punishment is not effective. If a teacher uses violence to solve problems in the classroom, then students will learn to use violence. Also, students who receive corporal punishment learn to hate their teacher. How can you learn from someone you hate? Classrooms should be places of cooperation. How can a student cooperate with someone who is hitting them? The law should protect children from violence the same way the law protects adults from violence. Why is it ok to hit children, but it's not okay to hit adults? ❞

1. Please circle the main idea in each opinion.

2. Please underline the supporting ideas in each opinion.

3. What could you say to further support the opinion with which you agree?

Discussion Questions

● **Discuss the questions in groups.**

1. What kind of school produces better students - one that uses corporal punishment, or one that doesn't? Explain your answer.

2. What kind of corporal punishment is worse - from your parents or at school? Explain your answer.

3. What do you think about the trend away from corporal punishment in North America? Is it kinder, or just weak? Explain your answer.

4. If you were in charge of discipline at your school, would there be corporal punishment? When would you use it? Would you use alternative punishments?

5. Is it more important to like your teachers and parents, or to respect their authority? Explain your answer.

Expression Tips
Informative Expressions
Furthermore, ~
I heard that ~
I'd like to add something to it.
In addition, ~

Time to Debate

Choose one statement. Debate the statement in groups.
(One group agrees with the statement, the other group disagrees with the statement.)

1. Violence does not encourage education.

2. Sometimes corporal punishment is necessary.

3. It takes time and patience to change bad behavior.

UNIT 15 The Lottery

Warm-up

● **1. List things you would do if you won the lottery.**

> go on a trip around the world,

2. What are some things that you can't buy?

> love,

● **Interview a classmate using the questions below.**

1. How much money can you win in the lottery right now?
2. What's the first thing you would do if you won the lottery?

The Lottery

🟠 **Read the passage.**

Track 43

More than 70 countries have national lotteries where citizens buy tickets for a chance to be rich. In many of these countries the lottery is operated by the government. Of all the money paid in tickets, only half goes to the winners. The government keeps the other half and spends it on roads or schools.

This money helps governments improve their countries in many ways. Without it, many useful things would never be built or fixed. People might have to pay more taxes to pay for improvements. With lotteries, people spend the money when they feel they can afford it.

The biggest payoff for a single ticket happened in Nebraska, USA in 2006. Eight people who worked at a meat processing factory won more than 365 million dollars. The newspapers often print stories about lottery winners. This usually makes people want to buy more lottery tickets.

The chances of winning a lottery are extremely bad. Usually, players select 6 numbers from the numbers 1 through 49. They can have a machine pick the numbers or choose the numbers themselves. In this format, the chances of winning are 1 in 14 million. However, each person's chance is as good as another's.

There have been many studies on how winning the lottery changes people's lives. Some people can't adjust to becoming millionaires, making bad investments and wasting their money. Some go bankrupt!

Comprehension Check Answer the questions.

1. How many countries have national lotteries?
2. Who usually operates the lottery?
3. What was the biggest lottery winning ever?
4. What are the chances of winning the lottery when 6 numbers are chosen?
5. Does everyone adjust well to being a lottery winner?

Vocabulary Check Complete the sentence with a word from the box.

| citizen | payoff | adjust | investments | format |

1. It was hard for him to _____ to his new life as president.
2. We try not to make too many risky _____ with our money.
3. I'm an American _____ and I have the passport to prove it.
4. Make sure your assignments are printed in the correct _____ before you hand them in.
5. There's a big _____ if you win tonight's poker game.

Think About It

Think about the advantages and disadvantages of the lottery.

Advantages
- Raises money for important national projects
-
-

Disadvantages
- Causes poor people to waste money
-
-

Opinion Practice

● **Practice supporting/refuting the opinions.**

Supporting Opinions

1. Playing the lottery is not dangerous... _____
2. The lottery should be banned... _____
3. If you play the lottery you should buy more than one ticket... _____
4. The lottery is fun... _____

> a. because it will increase your chances of winning.
> b. because people can become addicted and lose a lot of money.
> c. because you only play when you can afford it and it is very cheap.
> d. because you have a chance to become a millionaire overnight.

Refuting Opinions

1. You should invest money in banks and property, not waste it on the lottery. _____
2. You should pick your own numbers; never let the computer choose for you! _____
3. You should buy many lottery tickets if you want to be a millionaire. _____
4. If you win the lottery you should share the money with your friends. _____

> a. No, it is your money and you can do whatever you want with it.
> b. I do not agree. The lottery is a very cheap way to try and be a millionaire, so why not try? And investing in banks and property can be dangerous, too.
> c. Actually, it does not matter how you pick your numbers because the chances of winning will always be the same.
> d. Buying many tickets will not guarantee that you become a millionaire. Even if you buy 1,000 tickets the chances of winning are very small.

Opinion Examples

- Read the opinions and answer the questions.

Track 44

❝ The lottery is like a tax on people who are bad at math. Our chances of winning the lottery are almost zero. So many people play and often there is only one big winner. Some people play the lottery every week and after years have nothing to show for it. It seems silly to me that so many people would throw their money away so just a few people could be rich. It would be much smarter to save the money you spend playing the lottery. Of course, you wouldn't be rich but it would be better than nothing. ❞

Opinion B

Track 45

❝ The lottery gives us something to look forward to. I like to imagine what I could do with a million dollars. It makes me feel good to think about how I could help people. It makes me feel good to imagine having such great luck! Everyone would want to be my friend. There's nothing wrong with spending just a few dollars on that kind of fun. I know the chances are slim, but that's not really the point. ❞

1. Please circle the main idea in each opinion.
2. Please underline the supporting ideas in each opinion.
3. What could you say to further support the opinion with which you agree?

Discussion Questions

● **Discuss the questions in groups.**

1. How would winning the lottery affect your friendships? Explain your answer.

2. The government makes money from the lottery. Most people who buy lottery tickets are poor. Is this fair? Why or why not?

3. How much money would it take to make a person completely satisfied? Is there ever enough? Explain.

4. Is gambling addiction a real problem? Explain why or why not.

5. Does the lottery take advantage of people? Explain.

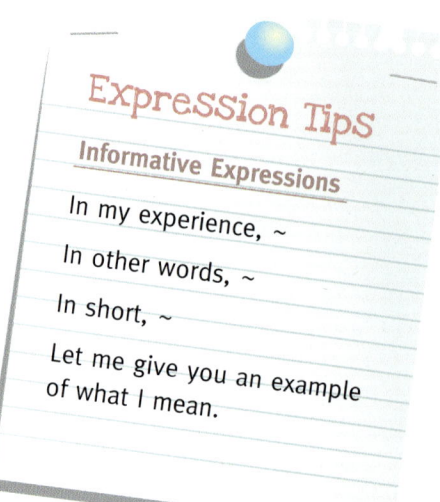

Expression Tips
Informative Expressions
In my experience, ~
In other words, ~
In short, ~
Let me give you an example of what I mean.

Time to Debate

Choose one statement. Debate the statement in groups.
(One group agrees with the statement, the other group disagrees with the statement.)

1. The lottery takes advantage of poor people and people with poor judgment.

2. The lottery is actually a good way to fund government projects.

3. The lottery is harmless, if you have no expectations.

UNIT 16 Gap between Rich and Poor

Warm-up

- Who makes the most money? Write high-paying jobs at the top of the triangle. Write low-paying jobs at the bottom.

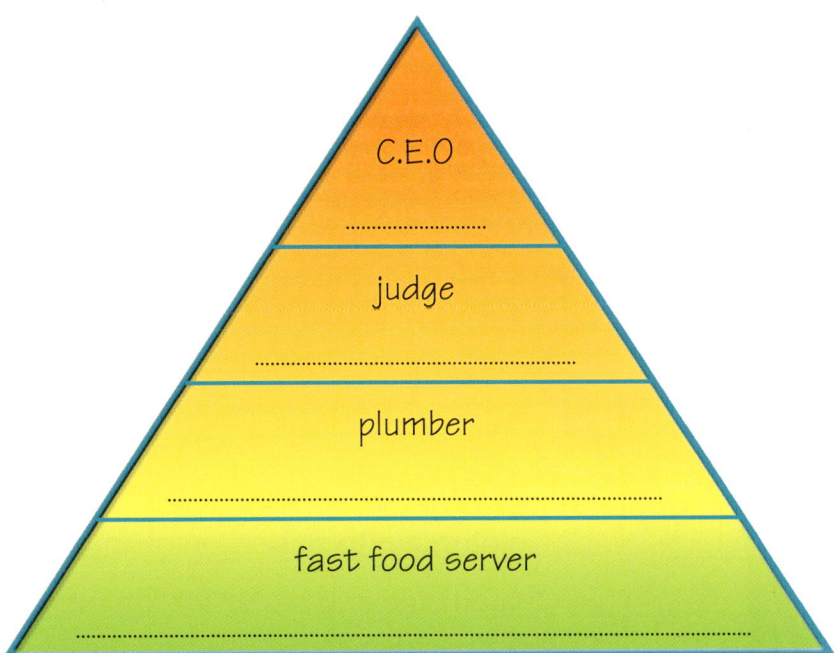

- Interview your classmates using the questions below.

  1. What are the basic things you need to survive?
  2. Do you think there are people in your neighborhood who can't afford those things?

Gap between Rich and Poor

🟠 **Read the passage.**

Track 46

A small part of the world's population is extremely rich. The richest 1% of the world's people own 40% of the world's assets. Much of the world is very poor. They can't afford food, medicine or clean water. The poorest half of the world's people own less than 1% of the world's assets.

That's a pretty unfair distribution of wealth. It's like one person in your class getting to eat 40 lunches and the rest of you having to share one lunch. If that happened, your teacher might ask him to share with the rest of you. After all, who needs 40 lunches?

But in the world economy, there's no solution that easy. There's no teacher that we'll all listen to, and the world is too big to control like a classroom.

Poverty affects people in many different ways. Mali is a country in Africa, and one of the world's poorest. In Mali, the life expectancy is 48 years. Only 26% of adults can read. Life is very hard for people in poor regions. They are trapped in a bad situation, and there's not very much they can do to change it.

Many aid organizations do try to help. People volunteer to raise money and get food, medicine and water for the poorest people. Some do it because they feel guilty. Others help because they believe they can change the world. Whatever the reason, help is needed every year in the world's poorest countries.

Comprehension Check   Answer the questions.

1. How many people own 40% of the world's assets?
2. How much of the world's asset do the poorest half of the world's people own?
3. Why do people volunteer?
4. What is the life expectancy in Mali?
5. What percentage of adults can read in Mali?

Vocabulary Check   Complete each sentence with a word from the box.

assets	distribution	poverty	expectancy	volunteered

1. It's hard to borrow money if you don't have any _____.
2. We don't have a lot of money, but we're not in _____.
3. The poorer a country is, the lower its life _____.
4. I _____ to help with the fundraiser on the weekend.
5. Is the _____ of food and medicine fair?

Think About It

Think about the advantages and disadvantages of international aid.

Advantages
- Saves the very poorest people from starving
-
-

Disadvantages
- Doesn't change the reasons those countries are poor
-
-

97

Opinion Practice

- **Practice supporting/refuting the opinions.**

   Supporting Opinions

   1. Rich people should help the poor… _____
   2. Rich people should not have to help the poor… _____
   3. Everyone should have the same amount of money… _____
   4. It is important to have money… _____

   > a. since we need to pay for food, housing and education. If we did not have money we could not have these things.
   > b. because the rich have so much and the poor have very little.
   > c. because rich people work hard for their money and deserve to keep it.
   > d. because all people are the same.

   Refuting Opinions

   1. Poor people should get a better job, then they can be rich. _____
   2. It is better to spend your money than to save it. _____
   3. Money is the most important thing in the world. _____
   4. Having money will make you happy. _____

   > a. It is not that simple. Poor people often have less education which makes it difficult to get a good job.
   > b. That is not true. It is more important to be happy and healthy than rich.
   > c. That is not necessarily true. Having money can also cause more problems.
   > d. Spending money can be fun, but it is important to save for emergencies in the future.

Opinion Examples

Read the opinions and answer the questions.

Opinion A

Track 47

" I believe that it is possible for one person to make a big difference in the world. Last week I read a story about a woman named Oprah Winfrey. She grew up in a very, very poor family. She had many hardships and few opportunities growing up. But she worked hard, and now she is one of the most famous and richest people in the world. She donates millions of dollars to help poor people around the world. She is just one person, and she made a big difference in many peoples' lives all over the world. "

Opinion B

Track 48

" The world's problems are really complicated, but some people think we can make a difference. They must be kidding! Putting a few quarters in a donation jar isn't going to make a difference. We're just a handful of people; what can we do? I think it's better to focus on your own life and your own problems. Then at least you have a chance of changing something. It's hard to accept, but there will always be poor people and rich people. Making donations won't change the way the world works, so don't kid yourself. "

1. Please circle the main idea in each opinion.

2. Please underline the supporting ideas in each opinion.

3. What would you say to further support the opinion with which you agree?

Discussion Questions

● **Discuss the questions in groups.**

1. Do you think most people care about poverty? Why or why not?

2. Do you think it's fair that some have so much and others have so little? Why or why not?

3. How would your life be different if you were poor? Give several examples.

4. What could be done to help make the world fairer?

5. Whose job is it to solve economic problems? Politicians? Charities? Us?

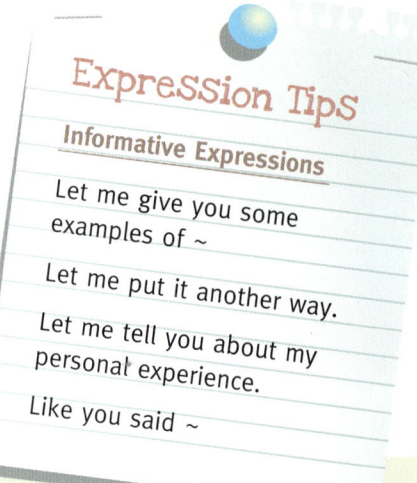

Expression Tips
Informative Expressions
Let me give you some examples of ~
Let me put it another way.
Let me tell you about my personal experience.
Like you said ~

Time to Debate

Choose one statement. Debate the statement in groups.
(One group agrees with the statement, the other group disagree with the statement.)

1. If people want more money, they just need to work harder.

2. The government should give money to people who are poor.

3. The world's richest people should share their wealth with the poor.

UNIT 17 Modern Life

ED1-17
MP3

Warm-up

● Fill in the chart with things that would have been more difficult in the past.

Challenges from the past	Reasons why challenging

Fill in the chart with things that would have been better in the past.

Things that were better in the past	Reasons why they were better

● Interview your classmates using the questions below.

1. What would you rather give up, television or computer? Why?
2. What would you do for fun if there were no computers or television?

101

Modern Life

🟠 **Read the passage.**

Track 49

So many things are fast and easy these days. You can send your thoughts to someone in an instant or heat up your food in a minute with a microwave oven. You can talk to your friend while she's riding in a car and you're at school. This may not sound like anything new, but computers, microwaves and cell phones have changed the way we live a lot in the past 30 years.

Some people say that modern life has brought too much stress. They say that the faster things change, the more stress we experience. In the past, it took many years to make things a little faster or easier. Today, change is quicker than ever before.

In 1925 there was no TV and certainly no computer. People had to wash the dishes by hand and do many chores. What would they do with the rest of their evening? They might listen to the radio. The radio was new and popular in the 1920s. Families would gather and listen to the radio. They found it amazing and exciting to hear voices coming out of it.

70 years later, people began using the internet. The 1990s changed the way people learn and have fun. Today everyone is busy texting, emailing or playing video games. There's no time for something as old-fashioned as sitting around the living room together. Is life really better now? For most of us, it's all we know. It's almost impossible to imagine life any other way.

Comprehension Check — Answer the questions.

1. According to the passage, what devices have changed our lives a lot in the past 30 years?
2. When did the radio become popular?
3. How were dishes washed in the past?
4. What's one bad side effect of change?
5. When did people start using the internet?

Vocabulary Check — Complete each sentence with a word from the box.

| modern | certainly | chores | amazing | old-fashioned |

1. _____ inventions like computers make our lives easier.
2. After you finish your _____, you can go play outside.
3. Riding horses is _____, but it's also fun.
4. I have _____ enjoyed spending the weekend with you.
5. We all found the magician's performance _____.

Think About It

Think about the advantages and disadvantages of modern life.

Advantages
- Many things are easier to do.
-
-

Disadvantages
- More stress
-
-

103

Opinion Practice

● **Practice supporting/refuting the opinions.**

Supporting Opinions

1. People should not use cell phones when driving... _____
2. We should continue to develop new types of energy... _____
3. The internet is the most important modern technology... _____
4. Our lives are easier than the lives of our grandparents... _____

> **a.** because it makes communication easier and provides fast access to information.
>
> **b.** because we have technology which makes work and communication faster.
>
> **c.** because it is dangerous for other drivers and it can cause an accident.
>
> **d.** because we cannot rely on fossil fuel forever.

Refuting Opinions

1. The internet is interesting; books are not. _____
2. It is more fun to play a soccer video game than to play real soccer. _____
3. Life is better today because of technology. _____
4. Listening to live music is better than listening to a CD. _____

> **a.** That is not true. There are books about every subject that you might be interested in and you can also read entertaining stories.
>
> **b.** That is not necessarily true. Many things are faster, but our lives are also busier and more stressful because of technology.
>
> **c.** Not anymore! Technology is so good today that when you listen to a CD it sounds better than the real thing.
>
> **d.** No way! It is better to be active and playing sports outside than to sit inside playing a video game all day.

Opinion Examples

● **Read the opinions and answer the questions.**

Track 50

❝ I think that all of our modern conveniences make our lives better than the lives of our ancestors. People live longer today because of medicines and advances in health care. Also, we have greater access to food and clean water, which makes us healthier. Machines like cars and planes allow us to travel great distances very quickly. Phones allow people today to communicate quickly and easily. In the past, it could take weeks to send someone a message in the mail or travel to another country. ❞

Opinion B

Track 51

❝ It seems like no matter how much we accomplish, we never get any happier. I don't think all these conveniences actually make our lives better. They just make our lives faster. We grow more impatient, wanting everything to happen in an instant. If we can't have it right now, we don't want it. I think what we really need is a sense of community. In the past, people relied on each other more. They were close because they needed each other in order to survive. Maybe they were difficult days, but at least everyone had a sense of purpose. ❞

1. Please circle the main idea in each opinion.

2. Please underline the supporting ideas in each opinion.

3. What would you say to further support the opinion with which you agree?

105

Discussion Questions

● **Discuss the questions in groups.**

1. Do the benefits of modern technology outweigh the problems? Why or why not?

2. Should there be laws requiring new technology to be environmentally friendly? Why or why not?

3. Modern medicine can make people live longer and longer. How long should a person live? Why?

4. What is the most important invention in the last 200 years? Explain your choice.

5. Should paper books be eliminated completely? Why or why not?

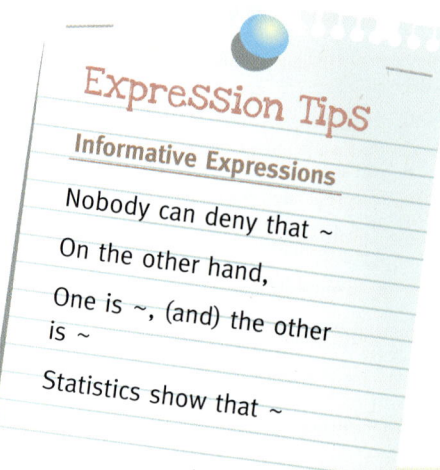

Expression Tips

Informative Expressions

Nobody can deny that ~

On the other hand,

One is ~, (and) the other is ~

Statistics show that ~

Choose one statement. Debate the statement in groups.
(One group agrees with the statement, the other group disagree with the statement.)

1. It's rude to talk on your cell phone while you're at the table.

2. *Facebook* is a really great way to keep in touch with people.

3. Life is no more stressful now than it was in the past.

UNIT 18 Animal Testing

Warm-up

- In the past all of these products were tested on animals. Did you use them today? Please answer Yes/No and fill in the table.

Product	How often do you use it?	If this product was bad, what might it do?
Toothpaste	Every day when I brush my teeth.	give me gum problems
Soap		
Washing detergent		
Cold and flu medicine		

- Interview a classmate using the questions below.

   1. Have you ever taken medicine? Explain why you needed to take it.
   2. Do you like animals? Explain why or why not.

Animal Testing

● Read the passage.

Our lives have benefited greatly from animal testing. It helped us discover vaccines for deadly diseases such as polio and measles and is currently helping to find treatments for cancer patients. Surgeries on animals have led to developments in organ transplants and open-heart surgery techniques. Animal testing has even given us new shampoos and cosmetic products to make us look beautiful.

Animal testing does have problems. It is estimated that one-hundred million animals are tested every year. Some experiments can be very painful, and usually the animals are killed after the experiment is finished, if the experiment itself does not kill them. Often, it does. The animals are not free to live a normal life. It is also possible that the results of the experiments will be misleading because of differences between animals and humans. Caring for and feeding these animals is also very expensive.

Those who support animal testing note that almost all of the medical achievements of the last 100 years are the result of experiments on animals. Opponents of animal testing argue that it is cruel and unethical to experiment on animals. They believe that the benefits to humans do not justify the suffering caused to animals and that the results of the experiments may be useless anyway.

Comprehension Check — Answer the questions.

1. How many animals are tested each year?
2. What happens to the animals after the experiment is finished?
3. How has animal testing helped doctors?
4. Animal testing helped find vaccines for many diseases. Name two of them.
5. Why do people oppose animal testing?

Vocabulary Check — Complete the sentence with a word from the box.

| cosmetics | estimate | vaccine | controversial | opponents |

1. Our team won the game. Our _____ lost.
2. Animal testing is a very _____ issue.
3. I wear many _____ to make my skin more beautiful.
4. I _____ that you are 165cm tall.
5. I don't want my dog to get sick, so I will give him a(n) _____.

Think About It

Think about the advantages and disadvantages of animal testing.

Advantages
- Can help cure diseases
-
-

Disadvantages
- Results may be misleading
-
-

109

Opinion Practice

- **Practice supporting/refuting the opinions.**

Supporting Opinions

1. Animal testing should be banned... _____
2. We should continue animal testing... _____
3. Animals should not be forced to live in a cage... _____
4. We should buy cosmetics that are not tested on animals... _____

> a. because the results of these tests help to make our lives better.
>
> b. because it is wrong to make animals suffer.
>
> c. since they need space to move. Animals should be free to run, fly, swim and climb.
>
> d. because we can look beautiful without hurting animals.

Refuting Opinions

1. Scientists are evil for hurting innocent animals. _____
2. It is OK to experiment on animals because they don't feel pain. _____
3. Humans are better than all other animals because we are smart. _____
4. It is OK for animals to suffer if it helps humans. _____

> a. That's not necessarily true. Birds can fly and fish can live underwater; humans cannot.
>
> b. That is ridiculous. Animals do get hurt and feel pain. That is why veterinarians exist.
>
> c. I disagree. No animal, human or otherwise, should have to suffer for any reason.
>
> d. That is not true. Scientists do their experiments because they want to help people, which is a good thing.

Opinion Examples

Read the opinions and answer the questions.

Opinion A

Track 53

❝ Animal testing is not necessary! Today we have new technologies and very smart computers which can get the same results as tests on animals. Scientists are able to grow human skin in a laboratory, and testing this skin would provide more accurate results than testing animals. There are also very advanced computer models which can accurately predict how new medicines will be able to fight diseases. It is unethical to continue to hurt animals when alternative ways of research are available. ❞

Opinion B

Track 54

❝ Animal testing is necessary! The human body is very difficult to understand. Computers and technology cannot always help us, and it is too dangerous to test on humans. Other animals, like chimpanzees, are very similar to humans. We can test them first and know if a medicine or operation will be safe for humans. Without animal testing too many people would get hurt or die. ❞

1. Please circle the main idea in each opinion.
2. Please underline the supporting ideas in each opinion.
3. What would you say to further support the opinion with which you agree?

Discussion Questions

● **Discuss the questions in groups.**

1. Do you think it is OK for animals to suffer to benefit humans? Explain your answer.

2. If it is wrong to experiment on animals, is it also wrong to eat them?

3. Many people have pets. Is it wrong to keep a pet in your house?

4. Would it be OK to experiment on humans?

5. Technology is becoming more powerful every day. Will computers ever be able to replace animal testing?

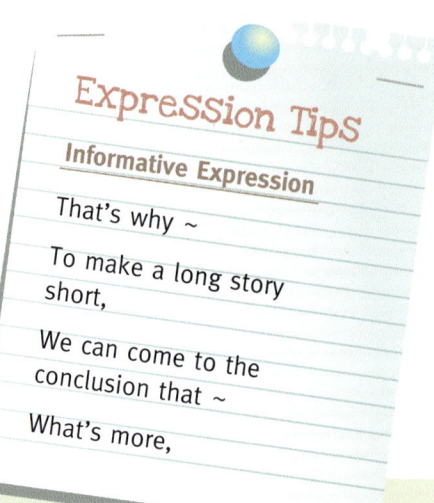

Expression Tips

Informative Expression

That's why ~

To make a long story short,

We can come to the conclusion that ~

What's more,

Time to Debate

Choose one statement. Debate the statement in groups.
(One group agrees with the statement, the other group disagrees with the statement.)

1. Using suffering to stop suffering is not ethical.

2. The benefits of animal testing far outweigh the costs.

3. In the future animal testing will continue to play a big part of our lives.

UNIT 19 Online Gaming

Warm-up

● Please fill in the table with information about any kind of game. Then use this information to answer the following questions.

Game	Who do you play with?	Do you play inside or outside?
Soccer	my friends and my team	outside on a soccer field
Starcraft	my friends or other people online	inside on a computer

● Interview a classmate using the questions below.

1. Do you play online games? How often do you play them?
2. What is your favorite online game? Explain why you like it.

Online Gaming

🟠 **Read the passage.**

Track 55

Online gaming is very popular with children and adults. Every day, millions of people connect to the internet to play games like *World of Warcraft* and *Starcraft*. You can play with friends or other people from all over the world, from the comfort of your home or a local PC room.

Not only is online gaming entertaining, it has many benefits, too! Many games involve complicated social networks. You must work with others to solve problems and accomplish tasks. You can learn from other players and develop friendships. These are vital life skills which we can use in everyday relationships. Reflexes can become quicker, and gamers usually score better on vision and problem solving tests than people who don't play online games.

Despite these benefits, excessive online gaming has been associated with many social and health problems. Doctors worry that people will become addicted, more violent, and less intelligent. It can lead to bad posture, wrist and neck soreness, back pain, and eye problems. It is also a leading cause of obesity, as excessive gamers are not very active. Critics believe that the time spent playing online games can be better spent studying, exercising, or meeting new people.

As computer technology and accessibility becomes greater, so will the popularity of online gaming. We must continue to examine the social and health effects of online gaming.

Comprehension Check — Answer the questions.

1. Why do doctors worry about excessive online gaming?
2. What do critics believe we should do instead of playing online games?
3. Who can you play online games with?
4. Gamers score well on what kinds of tests?
5. Why can excessive online gaming lead to obesity?

Vocabulary Check — Complete the sentence with a word from the box.

| critics | associated | posture | excessive | benefit |

1. The _____ do not believe that eating candy is healthy.
2. My back hurts because I have bad _____.
3. Eating too much food is _____ with obesity.
4. Finding a new, cheap source of energy would _____ everyone.
5. My teacher gave me too much homework. It was _____.

Think About It

Think about the advantages and disadvantages of online gaming.

Advantages
- Can make new friends
-
-

Disadvantages
- Can lead to obesity
-
-

115

Opinion Practice

- **Practice supporting/refuting the opinions.**

    Supporting Opinions

    1. Children should only spend a little time playing online games… _____
    2. You should do your homework before playing online games… _____
    3. Online games are better than board games… _____
    4. Teachers should use online games in schools… _____

    > a. because you can play with people all over the world.
    > b. because online games can help students learn and get better grades.
    > c. since playing excessively can lead to many health problems.
    > d. because it is important to learn new things and do well in school.

    Refuting Opinions

    1. Online gaming is only for children. _____
    2. If you play online games all day, you will have no friends. _____
    3. Playing online games will make you very smart. _____
    4. People will stop playing online games in the future. _____

    > a. No, it will not. Online games can teach you many important things, but if you want to be smart you must study, too.
    > b. I disagree. You can meet new people and make great friendships playing online games.
    > c. That's not true. Many adults enjoy playing online games, too.
    > d. I don't think so. As more people have computers online gaming will become more popular.

Opinion Examples

- **Read the opinions and answer the questions.**

Opinion A

Track 56

❝ Playing online games will make children less intelligent. If children play too many games they will not have time to do homework. Their grades will suffer and they won't be able to go to a good college or get a good job. Children should not spend all day playing games. It is a waste of time! Instead, they should study and learn new things. Playing games might be fun, but it is more important that they be smart. ❞

Opinion B

Track 57

❝ Playing online games can make children more intelligent. Scientific evidence has shown that children who play online games score well on tests. They are better at solving problems then people who don't play games. And not all online games are violent. Some are educational. Students can learn math and reading skills by playing online games. ❞

1. Please circle the main idea in each opinion.

2. Please underline the supporting ideas in each opinion.

3. What could you say to further support the opinion with which you agree?

Discussion Questions

● **Discuss the questions in groups.**

1. Online gaming can be very expensive. Do you think that it is OK to spend so much money playing online games?

2. Some people believe that excessive online gaming is the leading cause of child obesity. Is this true, or is there a more dangerous cause of child obesity?

3. How do your parents feel about online gaming? Do they play as well?

4. Online gaming is great because it allows you to play with people from all over the world. Do you think it is better to play with your friends, or to play with people online?

5. Some parents think it is not safe to let children play online games. Parents do not know who the other players are. They could be criminals. Is online gaming safe?

Expression Tips

Supporting Expressions

I admit that ~

I agree with ~

I am for ~

I couldn't agree with you more.

Choose one statement. Debate the statement in groups.
(One group agrees with the statement, the other group disagrees with the statement.)

1. Critics exaggerate the problems with online gaming. It is really just harmless fun.

2. Online gaming should be banned for anyone under the age of 18. Children should focus on learning, not games.

3. In the future everyone will own a computer, and everyone will play online games.

UNIT 20 Role Models

ED1-20
MP3

Warm-up

- Who are your role models? Write their names and explain why they are a positive or negative role model.

Name	Positive	Negative
Parents	They teach me about love and the importance of being a good person.	They do not listen to me. And make you do things that I do not want to do.

- Interview a classmate using the questions below.

  1. Who is your most important role model? Why did you choose that person?
  2. Do you have other role models, too? Who are they?

119

Role Models

🟠 **Read the passage.**

Track 58

A role model is a person we can look up to and base our character, values and aspirations on. Our first role models are our parents. They teach us everything about the world around us. We can look to them for help and guidance. As we get older, teachers and coaches show us that if we work hard we can be successful. Role models are everywhere. Unfortunately, we can learn good and bad, so we must choose our role models carefully.

Positive role models inspire us to succeed and be our best. They have worked hard, and many have overcome difficult obstacles. They teach us that with hard work we can achieve our goals despite the circumstances. For example, Barack Obama overcame racism to become President of the United States.

If children do not find positive role models, they may find bad role models. Negative role models inspire us towards bad things. Many of our favorite TV actors and superheroes are very violent and aggressive, and young boys try to be like them. Similarly, many successful female actresses and pop stars teach little girls that they must be beautiful if they want to be successful. This is a very unhealthy image for young children.

You will never be your role model, and that is a good thing. But our role models will help shape the persons we become, so it is important to choose our role models wisely.

Comprehension Check — Answer the questions.

1. What is one bad thing role models can teach young girls?
2. According to the passage, what do teachers and coaches teach us?
3. Who are our first role models?
4. Why is Barack Obama a positive role model?
5. What do positive role models do?

Vocabulary Check — Complete the sentence with a word from the box.

| aspiration | obstacles | overcame | character | values |

1. My baseball coach _____ hard work and teamwork.
2. Mary _____ many health problems to become a famous athlete.
3. John is nice and likes to help people. He has a good _____.
4. My _____ is to become a police officer.
5. The room was messy. I had to jump over many _____ to get to my bed.

Think About It

Answer the questions.

1. How has your life been affected by positive role models?

2. Do you think that superheroes like Batman and Superman are positive role models? Explain your answer.

3. Are you a role model? Do other people look up to you?

Opinion Practice

- **Practice supporting/refuting the opinions.**

   Supporting Opinions

   1. Our parents are our most important role models... _____
   2. Everyone should play team sports... _____
   3. Everyone should have a positive role model... _____
   4. Kobe Bryant is a great role model... _____

   > a. because he worked hard and became a successful basketball player.
   >
   > b. because they are the first people to teach us about the world.
   >
   > c. since positive role models inspire us to be our best.
   >
   > d. because coaches can teach us about hard work and cooperation.

   Refuting Opinions

   1. We can learn nothing from negative role models. _____
   2. Batman is a great role model because he fought evil people. _____
   3. You should not have a role model. It is better to be yourself. _____
   4. You should have the same role models as your friends. Then you will be cool. _____

   > a. I disagree. Negative role models can teach us things to avoid in our lives if we want to succeed.
   >
   > b. That is a bad idea. It is important to have role models who interest you. Do not worry about what your friends think.
   >
   > c. He teaches young children that it is OK to use violence to solve problems. He is a poor role model.
   >
   > d. You can be yourself and have a role model at the same time. They inspire us to be our best, but they do not make us different people.

Opinion Examples

- **Read the opinions and answer the questions.**

Track 59

❝ Coaches make great role models. They teach us that with hard work we can accomplish our goals. Also, in team sports our coaches help us to work together to succeed. Everyone should learn the importance of hard work and cooperation. They are skills which we can use in school, our jobs, and in our relationships with people. If we look to our coaches as role models we will be better prepared to become successful in life. ❞

Opinion B

Track 60

❝ It is dangerous to look at our coaches as role models. Coaches teach us that winning is the most important thing in life. If we do not win, then we are failures. Children might become aggressive and selfish. Also, they will not know how to deal with other types of failures in life, like getting a bad grade on a test. It is fun to win, but coaches should not make it the most important thing in sports. ❞

1. Please circle the main idea in each opinion.
2. Please underline the supporting ideas in each opinion.
3. What could you say to further support the opinion with which you agree?

Discussion Questions

● **Discuss the questions in groups.**

1. Do you think that it is better to have many role models, or only one?

2. Role models must be real people. Do you agree with this statement?

3. Would you like to be a role model when you are an adult?

4. A role model is the same as a hero. Do you agree with this statement?

5. Some people try to be exactly like their role model. They dress, talk, and act like them. Is this a good thing?

Expression Tips

Supporting Expressions

I have the same opinion about ~

I support ~

I totally agree with ~

I'm in favor of ~

Time to Debate

Choose one statement. Debate the statement in groups.
(One group agrees with the statement, the other group disagrees with the statement.)

1. Is it possible for someone to be a positive and negative role model at the same time?

2. Role models must be famous, successful people. No one else can be a role model.

3. People say that it is important to have a role model. Is it important? Explain why or why not.